(*TWAYNE'S WORLD AUTHORS SERIES* 305)

A Survey of the World's Literature

Sylvia E. Bowman, Indiana University

GENERAL EDITOR

POLAND

Irene Nagurski

EDITOR

Cyprian Norwid

TWAS 305

Cyprian Norwid

Cyprian Norwid

By George Gömöri

Darwin College, University of Cambridge

Twayne Publishers, Inc. :: New York

Library of Congress Cataloging in Publication Data

Gömöri, George, 1934–
    Cyprian Norwid.

    (Twayne's world authors series, TWAS 305. Poland)
    Bibliography: p. 155.
    1. Norwid, Cyprian, 1821–1883.
PG7158.N57Z64   891.8'5'16   73–17341
ISBN 0–8057–2656–X

To my Polish Friends

Contents

About the Author

George Gömöri is Lecturer in Polish at the University of Cambridge and Fellow of Darwin College. A native of Hungary, he has studied at Budapest and Oxford, was Lecturer at the University of California, Berkeley for one year, and in 1964–65 was Research Fellow at Harvard. He has been doing research on Norwid since the early sixties and has published essays on particular aspects of Norwid's work in such reviews as the *California Slavic Studies* and *The Slavonic and East European Review*, London. He has translated many of Norwid's poems into Hungarian.

Mr. Gömöri has written extensively on contemporary East European literatures. He is the author of *Polish and Hungarian Poetry 1945 to 1956*, Oxford: Clarendon Press, 1966, and co-editor of the anthology *New Writing of East Europe*, Chicago: Quadrangle, 1968, as well as of recent selections of modern Hungarian poets in English—Attila József, László Nagy. He has written chapters for *Crowell's Handbook of Contemporary Drama*, New York: Thomas Y. Crowell, 1971, and *World Literature Since 1945*, New York: Frederick Ungar, 1973. Mr. Gömöri is a contributor to such journals as *Survey*, *Tri-Quarterly*, *Mosaic* and *Books Abroad*. In 1972 he won the Jurzykowski Award for translation.

Preface

This is the first full-length study on the outstanding Polish poet and thinker Cyprian Norwid for the English-speaking reader. It has two interrelated but modest aims. First of all it tries to provide a sketch of Norwid's biography sufficient for the understanding of his work and the discussion of his achievement in each literary genre, with the main emphasis on poetry. Naturally most attention is paid to Norwid's major or pioneering works, since until now only a handful of his poems, some letters, and two short stories have been translated into English. A two-volume edition of his selected writings due to be published soon under the auspices of the University of Iowa will certainly improve the situation and is bound to be useful to anyone interested in Norwid but lacking a sufficient command of Polish to read him in the original, a task not considered easy even by native Poles, as Norwid uses the language with brilliant inventiveness.

My second aim is to give at least some idea of Norwid's thought and historiosophy while indicating his connections with Christian tradition and nineteenth-century European thought. The size of the book makes it impossible to follow up these connections and discuss them in detail. In some cases I present only my conclusions or the conclusions of other scholars without reconstructing the logic of the research that led to it.

Norwid's poetic and prose texts are quoted in my own English versions which—needless to say—cannot do justice to the vigor and complexity of the original. In the few cases where I used other English versions, the name of the translator is given after the quoted text.

I would like to express my thanks to the institutions whose support enabled me to write this book: first of all, the generosity of the Harvard Russian Research Center created for me the ideal preconditions of studying Norwid in the peace and quiet of the Widener Library. The cooperation of the British Council and the Literary Research Institute (IBL) of the Polish Academy of Sciences gave me the opportunity to do research in Warsaw libraries and archives in 1969. I was encouraged to write this book by Professor Czesław Miłosz of Berkeley and had useful conversations with Dr. J. W. Gomulicki and Dr. Zofia Stefanowska. Finally, I would like to thank Dr. Gerald Stone for reading the manuscript and making valuable comments on it.

GEORGE GÖMÖRI

Darwin College, University of Cambridge

Chronology

1821 Born September 24 in Laskowo-Głuchy near Radzymin.
1831 Enrolls in a Warsaw high school (*gymnasium*).
1837– Studies fine arts in Warsaw.
1838
1840 First poems printed in Warsaw reviews.
1841– Social and poetic success in Warsaw, contacts with young
1842 Bohemians and plotters, trips to the countryside with
      Władysław Wężyk.
1842 In September leaves Poland for Germany.
1843– Studies sculpture and art history in Florence. Visits Rome
1844 and Naples.
1845 Studies archaeology in Rome. Social contacts with Maria
      Kalergis. In the autumn a short stay in Silesia, then pro-
      ceeds to Berlin.
1846 Arrested in Berlin for having given away his passport to a
      deserter from the Russian Army. At the end of July a trip
      to Brussels where he meets émigré circles.
1847– Lives in Rome. Very active both as a painter and a poet.
1848 The first version of *Wanda* completed. Friendly relations
      with Krasiński. Active interest in politics; public clash with
      Mickiewicz. Boat tour of the Mediterranean.
1849 Leaves Rome for Paris. Introduced to Prince Czartoryski,
      Słowacki, and Chopin. The publication of *Wigilia* and
      Jeszcze słowo in Paris, *Pieśń społeczna* in Poznań.
1850– Financial problems, illness, partial deafness. *Promethidion*
1852 and *Zwolon* are published; both meet hostile criticism.
      Completes *Krakus* and the second version of *Wanda*. Po-
      litical and esthetic differences lead to a break with Kra-
      siński. A final rupture with Maria Kalergis.

1853– Sails from England for New York where he works for the
1854 memorial album of the Universal Exhibition. In July, 1854, returns to England.
1855– In Paris, earns his living by diverse artistic work. *Black*
1856 *Flowers* (*Czarne kwiaty*) is printed in the review *Czas*.
1857 *White Flowers* (*Białe kwiaty*) is published; *Quidam* is completed.
1859 Writes two poems about John Brown.
1860 Public lectures on Słowacki.
1861 Lectures on Słowacki published; writes *Civilization* (*Cywilizacja*).
1862 *Poems* (*Poezje*) is published by Brockhaus in Leipzig.
1863– Follows the uprising in Poland with passionate interest,
1864 writes articles, sends memoranda to the National Committee. Sends *Slavery* (*Niewola*) to Brockhaus.
1865 *Vade-Mecum* is completed. Writes *Chopin's Piano* (*Fortepian Szopena*).
1866– All efforts to get *Vade-Mecum* published fail. Paints a
1867 large canvas for the Saint Casimir Asylum. New financial difficulties.
1869 Friendship and love affair with Zofia Węgierska. Public reading of *A Poem about the Freedom of the Word* (*Rzecz o wolności słowa*), later published as separate booklet. Węgierska's sudden death.
1870– Starts work on *Assunta*. During the siege of Paris and the
1871 Commune he is starving, his health deteriorates.
1872 Writes *The Ring of a Grand Lady*, works on *Cleopatra and Caesar*.
1876 Plans of moving to Italy.
1877 Financial difficulties force him to live in the Saint Casimir Asylum, a Polish home for the aged.
1883 Writes *Ad leones!* and *Lord Singleworth's Secret* (*Tajemnica lorda Singleworth*).
1883 Norwid dies on May 23. Buried at Ivry two days later.
1888 His mortal remains are transferred to the Polish cemetery at Montmorency.
1901 The first number of *Chimera*, a literary review edited by Przesmycki in Warsaw inaugurates Norwid's gradual rediscovery.

CHAPTER 1

The Young Norwid

I Lyric Poems: The Warsaw Period

CYPRIAN Norwid was nineteen years old when his first published poem appeared in the literary supplement of a Warsaw journal. He must have been writing poetry for some time, since his first printed (though anonymous) poem bore the title *My Last Sonnet*. With the exception of *Loneliness,* another sonnet perhaps written earlier but published almost simultaneously, the rest of the sonnets have not been preserved; it is not impossible that the poet himself destroyed them some time later. *My Last Sonnet* was published in February, 1840, and during the same year a few more of Norwid's poems appeared. They won quick critical acclaim in Warsaw and even in Petersburg, where the critic of a Polish-language newspaper made favorable comments on the poems published "with the signature C.N."

As a matter of fact, Norwid was never so much in favor with the critics as in the first two years of his poetic career. His poems printed in the fashionable literary and cultural reviews of the period, such as *The Warsaw Review* (*Przegląd Warszawski*) or the newly founded *Warsaw Library* (*Biblioteka Warszawska*), attracted much friendly and in some cases enthusiastic attention. There is more than one reason to account for this. These early poems were—for all their obscure allusions and brooding secretiveness—easy to grasp, and their mood was fashionable with the educated reader. Since the Romantic breakthrough in the eighteen-thirties, melancholy and a kind of Byronic *Weltschmerz* were accepted as an essential constituent part of the poet's world; besides, Brodziński, Malczewski, and the young Mickiewicz had left an imprint on the tastes of the next generation of writers.

Another reason for Norwid's popularity could be found in the young poet's traditionalism. His poems written between 1840 and 1842 show Norwid as a deeply religious person who is dismayed by the imperfection of reality and by the enormity of human suffering which seems to be an integral part of life. In one poem he denounces the power of money in an emotional outburst while in another he declares his love for the village and his hostility to urban life with its din, smoke, and false glitter. This poem, incidentally, *Remembering the Village* (*Wspomnienie wioski*) was his most popular piece at the time, for it captured and expressed the nostalgic longing of the ex-landowner, the gentry, and the impoverished nobleman for what they regarded as their "lost heritage." City life for Norwid is full of uncertainty and lurking evil, while the simplicity and kindness of village life is idealized in glowing terms: "Village! . . . that's my life, God's gift it is! / It is a flower that falls from an angel's hair . . ." [1]

Norwid's family background partly explains his enthusiasm for the village: he himself was born in the country and lived there until the age of nine. Coming from a family of impoverished nobility, neither he nor his father felt really at home in Warsaw. On the other hand, *Remembering the Village* expressed the mood of other young intellectuals and writers as well: an early novel of Józef Kraszewski *The Poet and the World* (*Poeta i świat*) voices very similar sentiments to those of Norwid. Finally, those were the years when the Romantic interest in folklore turned into a cult of the people—the village folk. Young scholars began to observe and describe popular customs, to explore a way of life thitherto unknown. Norwid's populism, if somewhat naive, fitted into this pattern, too. In his later years his admiration for the serenity and unruffled calm of the Polish village underwent certain qualifications; witness such works as *A Dorio ad Phrygium*.

However, not everything that Norwid wrote in his Warsaw years was conventional. The fact that he did not write anything overtly political did not mean an aloofness from politics. The crude political oppression following in the wake of the 1830 uprising and the Russian-Polish war could not fail to impress the mind of the young poet. Not that he was a radical; he refused to follow the example of revolutionary firebrands like the poet Gustaw Ehrenberg or the ill-fated young plotter Karol Levittoux. Norwid was opposed to revolutionary plotting both for pragmatic and Christian reasons and years later publicly questioned the necessity of "the periodic massacre of innocents" resulting from the failure of innumerable conspiracies and untimely risings. Nonetheless, he was deeply touched by the fate of his friends and colleagues exiled to Siberia or sent to the gallows by the Tsarist authorities. His early poems are interspersed with images alluding to the torments of his persecuted and martyred friends. In one of the best pieces of this period *Night in the Desert* (*Wieczór w pustkach*) he speaks about the kind of silence which sets in before a public execution: "This occurs when a martyr / is dragged to be put to death" and on such occasions "people learn / to die in a Christian way." [2] According to one interpretation, another poem from these years, *The Storm* (*Burza*), contains "disguised praise of the young patriot and martyr Karol Levittoux and makes a clear allusion to his suicidal death." [3] Some months before this poem was written Levittoux was arrested and interrogated: the authorities hoped to eliminate his whole organization. In order not to give away any names Levittoux chose suicide which, imprisoned in the Fortress of Warsaw, he could commit only in a particularly painful and macabre manner, by burning himself alive. From Krasiński's letter to Delfina Potocka we know that the martyrdom of Levittoux, whom Norwid knew personally, remained one of the young and sensitive poet's most shattering experiences.

Following this line of thought, it is perhaps justified to attribute Norwid's predilection for allegories and parabolic expression to the political realities of this period. While trying to communicate his sadness and horror over oppression and its deplorable consequences for his generation, Norwid avoided direct references for both political and artistic reasons. At this time he found all forms of declarativeness distasteful; moreover, while still in Warsaw Norwid began to reflect upon the function of *silence* or *pause* in the work of art, a problem that in his more advanced years became the axis of his esthetic theory. In one of his first published poems he praised "the charm and delight of silence," in *Night in the Desert* going further: ". . . and hardly anyone knows / That sometimes it is a hundred times better to converse / With *Silence* than with a man." [4] This poem shows, incidentally, that apart from conspiratorial reasons Norwid relished silence as the natural background to meditation, which in turn would lead to minute observations of poetic significance.

Silence, loneliness—could these be the key words to the Warsaw period in Norwid's poetry? Not if we consider all his poems and his way of life. The young poet was seen in smoke-filled suburban inns in the company of gay Bohemians and in Warsaw salons alike. His poems were printed, quoted, and admired; his talents recognized. Inevitably he was also envied and disliked, especially by those of "democratic" leanings who criticized Norwid for his "dandyism" and "lack of solidarity" with his peers. His reserve was taken for arrogance; his cleanliness and selective taste for pseudoaristocratic hauteur. Though he shared the interests and some of the aspirations of his generation, it was clear to the contemporary observer that he did not really belong to the *Cyganeria,* a group of artistic-literary Bohemians, and could not embrace their radical politics. He did not belong to the world of the salons either, being neither rich, nor very ambitious to make a career. His charm and good manners were appreciated, and he was accepted as a promising artist and poet, but not as a potential suitor for any of the young ladies. The early death of his father and the modest material means at his disposal made Norwid's social status and future uncertain. One could rebel against this future, or one could accept it in a Christian spirit of sacrifice and resignation. The latter approach nevertheless implied "silence" and the "loneliness" of nonidentification with either class or group. In this sense Norwid's future is already written into the social experiences of the Warsaw years.

In May, 1842, Norwid got his passport and was permitted to leave the Congress Kingdom (the Russian-administered part of Poland) in order "to perfect himself in the art of sculpture." His wanderings through the Polish countryside with his fellow poet and friend Władysław Wężyk must have whetted Norwid's appetite for more travel. As for his studies of fine art, probably his first teacher, Minasowicz, encouraged his artistic ambitions and pointed out to him the importance of further study abroad. Minasowicz himself had studied in Paris and Rome and returned to Warsaw only in 1835. Art gave the pretext to get away from the provincial and politically oppressive atmosphere of Warsaw, but Norwid did not contemplate emigration: only a few months before his departure he became engaged to be married. He planned to spend a few years in Italy and then return home. Still, his departure was quite an event. His poet-friends turned out to say farewell to him in full force, and his trip abroad was deemed important enough to be mentioned even by the correspondent of the *Revue des Deux Mondes*.[5] Norwid left Warsaw by coach—never to return again.

II *In Italy*

The first poem written by Norwid after leaving his native country was in a sense prophetic. It was inspired by a visit to the Lorenzkirche in Nurenberg where he saw and admired a font by the medieval artist Adam Krafft. The artist who created this masterpiece was not appreciated in his lifetime and died in great poverty. For Norwid, Krafft's fate gained a symbolic depth. Great artists are often slighted by their contemporaries, but this does not diminish the value of their work. From Norwid's poem it seems as if only the unappreciated artist has the right to call himself an artist at all. Krafft is addressed in these words:

> Oh great master! you gave an example
> Towards what paths others should make their way. . . .[6]

This sounds as if Norwid would have consciously chosen the role of the unpopular artist whose struggle for self-realization is a constant challenge to society. Or else the poem on Krafft is an intimation of Norwid's own artistic credo: find your own way, never curry favor with the public, turn your back on fashion. Later, this uncompromising attitude to the expectations of his readers became an important, if not the most important, source of Norwid's loneliness and increasingly bitter isolation.

After a sojourn in Dresden and Munich the young Polish artist arrived in Italy during the early spring of 1843. From Venice he proceeded to Florence where he began his studies of painting at the Academy of Fine Arts, and of sculpture under the Italian master Pampaloni. The next two years spent in intensive reading, studying, and traveling were among the happiest in Norwid's life, being also the most formative years in which his esthetic ideals took definite shape. Many ideas appearing in a crystallized form only later in the poems, dramas, and essays of the 1847–1851 period have their root in the visual and intellectual experiences that Italy gave to the young painter and poet. He read Dante, Michelangelo, and Tasso, visited Fiesole, Perugia, Pompeii, and Rome, discovering the miracle of Mediterranean art which is so firmly rooted in history and social reality and yet has a way of communicating values that are seemingly eternal.

An important year in Norwid's life was 1844: it marked his coming of age as a poet and thinker. This was a painful process as it involved a drastic revision of some youthful dreams and ideals to which he had adhered previously. *To My Brother Ludwig* (*Do mojego brata Ludwika*), a poem written in Florence, shows a disillusionment somewhat out of proportion to the event that provoked it—the news from Poland that Kamilla L. was breaking her engagement to Norwid to marry someone else. Norwid was prompted to brood over the instability of worldly things: "How few things are certain on this earth / One can throw ashes on anything sweet . . . ," and to conclude that he could not have trust in "happiness" any more. His disappointment was put forward even more forcefully, without any philosophical commentary, in *My Song (I)*, (*Moja piosenka, I*), a typically Romantic statement of despair:

> I am sad, I am sad always and everywhere.
> The black thread keeps spinning:
> She is behind me, in front of me, by my side,
> In every breath of mine
> And in every smile
> She is present in my tears, in the prayer
> and in the song divine. . . .[7]

It should be noted, however, that his fiancée's "betrayal" freed Norwid from the most important obligation that still bound him to Warsaw. Though he kept sending his poems to Warsaw reviews, some of these—like *To My Brother Ludwig*—seemed to puzzle the readers with their complexity and a certain obscurity of thought. Clearly, Norwid was grappling with the language, trying to find adequate expression for his recent emotional crisis and philosophical experiences. His growing interest in philosophy included a search for the meaning of human life in the past: his visit to Pompeii, studies of Etruscan art, and the close reading of Latin authors including the early Fathers of the Church, all pointed in this direction.

Between 1844 and 1846 Norwid did not write much poetry. He was preoccupied with the translation of some fragments of the *Divina Commedia* (this was the first manuscript of the young

The Young Norwid

Norwid that later fell into the hands of Zygmunt Krasiński) and
was absorbed in artistic work as well as taking part, mainly with
Polish friends, in philosophical and political discussions. His reputation as a promising artist and, above all, as a "wholesome"
young man persisted. Orpiszewski, Czartoryski's agent who met
him in Florence in 1844, described him in a letter as a man of
"quite unusual talents, very well-educated, with honorable feelings; he is prudent, religious and understands everything. . . ." [8]
Most people who met Norwid at this period were full of praise
and sympathy for him and, perhaps, this mood of general acceptance encouraged him when he met Maria Kalergis for the
first time. Madame Kalergis, the celebrated half-Russian beauty
of Warsaw and a few years later of Paris society, had been living
apart from her rich Greek husband for some time and spent most
of her time abroad, meeting and being entertained by such celeb-
rities as Liszt, Chopin, and Gautier. She was beautiful in a cool,
Nordic fashion, as well as being well-educated and a good con-
versationalist. As soon as they met in the fall of 1844, Norwid
fell in love with her.

This was unfortunate, since his love remained, almost inevitably, unrequited. For Madame Kalergis the Italian encounter
with Cyprian Norwid was a fleeting episode; his response to her
charms a matter of little consequence. While the attentions of
the young artist probably amused or flattered her, she never took
him seriously. He was simply *le gamin,* a young man nice to have
around. He was allowed to keep the ladies company (Kalergis
usually traveled with her lady-in-waiting Maria Trębicka) for
an outing or some other social occasion, but when he began to
follow Kalergis and besiege her with spoken or unspoken declarations of love, he became a nuisance. At one point she must have
rejected him unambiguously, making him understand that he
stood no chance. According to one source [9] this final break happened in Venice in 1849—but in Norwid's correspondence we
meet Kalergis's name more than once after that date, so it is possible that the last humiliation was inflicted on Norwid only in
Paris. Never before or after did Norwid love anyone for so long,
nor did anyone ever deal such a blow to his pride and self-
esteem as Maria Kalergis. Apart from the lack of emotional response on the part of the "marble white lady," as Gautier dubbed
Kalergis, there were unsurmountable difficulties of a financial

[19]

kind; Norwid simply did not have the income to marry someone with Madame Kalergis's expensive tastes and demands.

The whole protracted drama of Norwid's disappointed love for Maria Kalergis found little direct expression in his poetry. A few short love poems written to Kalergis without name or dedication and a long correspondence with her confidante Trębicka—on the face of it nothing more remained of the whole affair. Still, no perspicacity is needed to establish that for many years to come Norwid was still suffering from the aftereffects. By nature a sensitive and proud introvert, after the break with Kalergis and her "extension" Trębicka, Norwid became even less willing to exhibit his sentiments; for the rest of his life he was reserved about his love affairs to the point of secretiveness. Had Zofia Węgierska's letters to Norwid been lost, we might have never learned about the intensity of feeling that bound the middle-aged Norwid to this attractive and brave woman: her name is not mentioned in any of Norwid's poems. His reticence and reluctance to declare his feelings openly did not prevent Norwid from airing his resentment toward a certain type of upper-class woman, the society lady whose glittering appearance hides a cool and calculated, or just indifferent, heart. His opinion about such ladies (among whom, no doubt, he counted the celebrated Madame Kalergis as well) was best expressed in these lines:

> And I have met women enchanted dead—
> Thousands of formulas—till I could cry
> At all that charm with all emotion fled
> As I transfixed them with a passionless eye. . . .[10]

III   Commitment and Conflict

Norwid's interest in social and political problems dates back to his Warsaw days. A close reading of his early poems shows that he shared the patriotism and grievances of the majority of Polish youth living under Russian occupation. In those days various personal, moral or esthetic considerations kept him back from active participation in politics, that is to say, from conspiracy. In 1845, however, when he went to Silesia to visit his old friend Władysław Wężyk, he met a certain Jatowtt, a deserter from the Russian army who was trying to escape farther West.

Norwid gave him some money, and in a moment of unusual and somewhat inconsiderate generosity he gave the man his own passport. When Jatowtt appeared in Paris with Norwid's passport, the Russian ambassador sent word to Berlin. Norwid, who was studying history of art and philosophy there, was summarily arrested by the Prussian authorities. He was also suspected of having contacts with Mierosławski, whose plans of armed uprising had been betrayed and who himself had been jailed only a few months earlier. There is some new evidence indicating Norwid's participation in, or at least knowledge of, the "Mierosławski conspiracy," for just at the time of the planned uprising he made a visit to the Duchy of Poznań.[11] The poet's imprisonment did not last long, thanks to the intervention of an influential aristocrat who secured his release, but those few days spent in the dark and humid prison cell left an infirmity which stayed with him for the rest of his life—a partial deafness which in later years grew worse and became increasingly hard to bear.

From Berlin Norwid proceeded to Brussels and spent some time by the sea in Ostende. In Brussels he established close contacts with émigré circles, met General Skrzynecki of 1830 fame and the famous historian Lelewel. Here he got involved for the first time in the political activities of the emigration. He was approached by, and promised support to, Czartoryski's followers with whom at this point he sympathized.

In the first months of 1847 he returned to Rome, probably because of the presence of Maria Kalergis, but apart from that, quite a few of Norwid's friends and acquaintances lived there. The Polish colony consisted mainly of artists, priests, and upperclass visitors from Poland. The lively discussions on art and literature taking place in numerous salons and ateliers played a vital part in the formulation of Norwid's own art theory. At this point he still regarded himself mainly as an artist—a painter who wrote poetry rather than the other way around. Apart from painting, he now tried his pen at a historical play entitled *Patkul*, which was later lost or destroyed by the poet himself. By the autumn of 1847, he had written the first version of the mystery play *Wanda*, a clear proof that his poetic strength was returning. Immersed in esthetic and historiosophic debates with his friends, Norwid did not neglect religious meditation. In the magnificent stage-setting of Rome, where one day he would visit the Colosseum and the next descend to the catacombs, Norwid experienced an upsurge of awe and deep respect for the early Christians who witnessed the collapse of a great civilization and were ready to die for their faith. This nucleus of faith Norwid considered the most valuable asset in Christianity; and he tried later to emulate in his life and work the silent heroism of Christ's first followers.

The year 1848 was full of challenge for Norwid. It gave him the first opportunities to participate in the political battles and confrontations of the day. Furthermore, the events of the year also stimulated his poetic vein to express views on a variety of social and national problems preoccupying the Polish political elite at the time. This he did in poems like *On the Eve (Wigilia)* and *One More Word (Jeszcze słowo)*, in the long epic poem entitled *Four Pages of a Social Song (Pieśni społecznej cztery stron)* and in the plays *Wanda* and *Zwolon*. Of all these the clearest expression of the young Norwid's social and political views can be found in the *Four Pages*, a long and openly didactic poem written in simple trochaic lines with an equally simple *abab* rhyme pattern.

Striking in this epic poem is the seriousness with which the poet approaches his subject matter. The *Four Pages of a Social Song* is divided into four parts entitled "Liberty, Equality, Fraternity," "Slavery," "Property," and "The Republic." Already these subtitles imply that Norwid's ambition was not so much to enchant the reader with the brilliance of his language or unexpected imagery as to convey a message. For example, his definition of freedom in the liberated Poland of the future reads as follows:

> There'll be a different freedom in Poland,
> it will be neither noble-golden,
> nor the communal thatched-roof freedom
> stretching from fence to fence,
> neither an abysmal-Slavonic kind
> pregnant with Tatar deeds,
> nor such a freedom about which
> the guillotine-mad Cabbalist dreams [12]

This could be read as a short list of those political attitudes which Norwid finds most objectionable. He cannot share the conservative nostalgia for the days of "golden freedom" and *liberum veto*—a concept which, incidentally, excludes the majority of the nation from the privileges of the nobility—though he, too, idealized the more distant Polish past. He has little sympathy for the Panslavic or the radical democratic concepts of social reform, but at the same time he refuses to accept and condone that peculiar sort of national mysticism that pervaded the ranks of the excitable, embittered, and frustrated generation of the so-called "Paskievich Era." Later, when Norwid was already in Paris, he was reported to have characterized the mood of the young emigration in words that almost defy translation as "thorny, palmaceous, dirty" (*cierniowo-palmisto-brudny*). Norwid's freedom based on "good will" is supposed to be reached through such orthodox Christian values as love, faith and hope. Both here and in another epic poem, *Slavery (Niewola)*, completed later, Norwid tried to define the meaning of freedom. He saw it not so much as a political or human right achieved by legislation, but as a process and a potentiality—the fullest possible enjoyment of man's creative powers, the complete and full participation in life by everybody: "Freedom is the universal utilization / of all the power life has" (*Wolność to jest wszechużycie Wszechpotęgi bytu . . .*).[13]

In the third part of the *Four Pages* there is a shift from politics and philosophy to something like a social program. Norwid here expounds his views on property which are old-fashioned in an attractive way. For him property is not so much the inalienable possession of an individual, as the "social use" of something that happens to belong to you. In other words, property has his approval as long as it is handled and used prudently and (this is the crux of the matter) conscientiously. Division of labor divides people into owners of property and owners of "time," and Norwid cannot see much wrong in that. Trouble starts when one group or the other begins to ignore its duties toward society: when the landowner treats the laborer unfairly and neglects to pay attention to the common good of the state, or when the havenots decide to rebel against the social order, thus disrupting the balance. "No property without conscience" is the key phrase in this part of the poem; property should entail social responsibility. Norwid sees the state and the nation as an organism and also as a channel through which the rich can make *conscientious use* of their wealth. The republic is ruined if it serves the interests of only one party, clique, or propertied class. It should rest on "the conscience of all" (*wielosumienie*).

This program would have been admirable in the sixteenth or seventeenth century when the *Rzeczpospolita*, the republic of the nobility, still flourished in Poland. Judging by his program, Norwid still thinks in terms of a patriarchal agrarian society; his concepts recall Latin authors or such important political thinkers of the sixteenth century as Andrzej Frycz-Modrzewski who, as Kridl says, "wished the republic to be reformed within the existing framework of her polity." [14] Yet in the middle of the nineteenth century and in the wake of the Galician revolt where peasants denounced and slaughtered their Polish masters with the active encouragement of the Austrian authorities, such a program was anachronistic and in some ways just naive. It did not take into account the diverse social forces which were slowly transforming the patriarchal way of life in partitioned Poland; neither did it pay any attention to the problem of industrialization and the new conflicts arising between the industrialist and the proletariat. Yet before 1848–1849 almost the entire Polish intellectual élite thought in these categories, believing that the "industrial problem" existed solely for the English and the French. For instance, Trentowski, Krasiński's philosopher-friend, maintained that the rise of the proletariat could be avoided in Poland, if only the national policy was "honest and conscientious." No wonder that Norwid, who at the time was close to Krasiński and his friends, shared some of their assumptions based on wishful thinking and ahistorical illusions.

While living in Rome, Norwid had established close contacts with Zygmunt Krasiński, the author of the *Undivine Comedy*, and not only his social but his political views were at that time influenced by the opinions of his immensely erudite and intelligent but also deeply neurotic and suspicious friend. Many barbs in the *Four Pages of a Social Song* were in fact directed against Adam Mickiewicz and the Towianists whom Krasiński, and also the religious order of *Zmartwychwstańców* or Resurrectionist order with whom Norwid also maintained good relations, regarded as their main political and spiritual enemies. The dramatic clash between Norwid and Mickiewicz at a Polish meeting in Rome where Norwid opposed the much older poet in the name of traditional Christian principles shows the extent of Norwid's engagement on the side of the conservatives or "moderates" within the emigration. Commenting on such obscurely prophetic poems of Norwid's written at the time as *On the Eve* (*Wigilia*) and *One More Word* (*Jeszcze słowo*), Juliusz Gomulicki suggests that "at that time Krasiński's philosophy was the main force behind Norwid's thought—he owed much of his ideas and poetic concepts to this philosophy." [15] This is certainly true of Norwid's political ideas, but his philosophy, even if it resembled Krasiński's views on many points, was the result of a long and autonomous process of thinking, including meditations over the relics of the past and the meaning of history throughout the ages. Such meditations imbued him with skepticism as to a rapid change of the world for the better and made him question the very notion of progress. As early as 1845 he wrote: ". . . another apparition scares me: / With every word the world is calling for *progress*, / With every dip of the pen. In short / It would not even agree on the alphabet. . . ." [16] In other words, even if "progress" is on everyone's lips, what constitutes progress? As there can be no agreement on this, the word has an empty ring.

This well-founded skepticism guided Norwid's actions in and around 1848. He volunteered for the Polish Legion formed by Mickiewicz but withdrew as soon as he understood the Panslavic and radical implications of Mickiewicz's program. While he certainly shared Cieszkowski's and Krasiński's belief in the Third Age (the Age of the Holy Spirit and universal brotherhood) and their hope in the resurrection of an independent Poland, the immediate future seemed to him blurred and full of potential setbacks and disasters. Perhaps he understood the lessons of history better than many of his compatriots, for he did not seem to share the Messianic expectations that swept through the Polish community in the early months of 1848. Both Krasiński and Mickiewicz expected a European war leading to the liberation of Poland; both were desperately waiting for a political or spiritual miracle to occur. The prolonged absence of this liberation turned Krasiński into a convinced counterrevolutionary and an enthusiastic supporter of "law and order."

Norwid took a more cautious view; the future, he explains in *On the Eve*, depends on God's plans, and at any rate it is futile to expect a Millenium just now (*Five Sketches*). A mock-Apocalypse is more likely to happen, bringing havoc upon the world but unable to solve the real problems of mankind. What Norwid feared most was premature action bringing counterproductive results. He was prepared to sacrifice his life for his principles but refused to squander it on outwardly heroic but senseless and hopeless ventures. In the revolutionary climate of 1848 and 1849, Norwid argued for patience and moderation, for an effort to understand the logic of history which was beyond most of his compatriots: "For is there any other nation in the world which has made so many premature sacrifices, involving so much blood, property and intellect?" [17] From this and other texts it appears that the danger of premature action is central in Norwid's political thinking. In this he is not so much a conservative as a dialectical thinker and a staunch believer in *organic* action. His conviction involves the rejection of ineffective and isolated plotting, resounding but useless declarations, and sporadic outbursts of individual terrorism. Neither Tsarist tyranny nor the injustice of Western industrial society can be remedied by theatrical gestures or the hasty application of half-baked economic theories. His attitude toward the Socialist movements of his days is expressed succinctly in *Times (Czasy)*, a poem written in 1849 and revised later, figuring in the *Vade-Mecum* cycle under the title *Socialism*. In this poem Norwid rejects the simplified contention of the Blanquists and other socialist-type movements of the 1840's, that there are "only *evil* ones and *chosen* ones" (emphasis in the original). He implies that the full realization of Socialist ideals is indeed a Titanic task, impossible to be achieved in the near future:

> Oh! History's work is not yet finished,
> Conscience has not yet burnt its way through the globe! [18]

This shift from enlightened conservatism to a new moral sensitivity and interest in the main issues of his age makes Norwid's poetry from 1849 onwards an interesting experiment not only in the context of Polish but of European literature as a whole.

CHAPTER 2

Promethidion

I *L'artiste inutile*

WHEN he arrived in Paris in February, 1849, Norwid was a
young artist in search of an audience. Whatever hopes he
attached to his move to Paris, he soon realized that although he
was welcome in most Polish salons as well as at political meetings
of the émigrés, no attention was paid to his poetic efforts, and
few, if any, paintings or sculptures were commissioned from him
by the émigré élite. At about the same time his name appeared
in *The Warsaw Courier* (*Kurier Warszawski*), the official publication of Russian-administered Poland, among those persons who
had left Poland without official authorization and were now regarded as "living in exile." This announcement placed Norwid
squarely into the category of political émigrés, a fate which he
had been prepared to accept ever since 1846. This, however, also
meant that henceforth he would be unable to get any financial
support from Poland. He had had material problems already in
Rome, but there Krasiński and other rich compatriots had helped
him with funds and minor commissions. Once in Paris, where his
friendship with Krasiński was subjected to severe strains and his
poetic and artistic work raised little interest in émigré circles,
Norwid's poverty became acute and the problem of physical survival a constant concern.

In a word, in these years between 1849 and 1852, Norwid began to give serious thought to his social status and predicament.
In Italy he had been a young artist living in modest circumstances
but moving in a circle of artists and aristocrats. Thanks to his
impeccable manners, fastidious dress, and, not least, his obvious
artistic talent, he had been accepted as a gentleman. In Paris he
was jolted into the realization that he was in fact an unemployed
intellectual. One of his drawings bears the title *l'artiste inutile*,

the unnecessary artist; in a poem he refers to himself as a "super-fluous actor" (*aktor nadkompletowy*). Almost overnight he found himself as one of the educated poor, an intellectual whose living standard was barely above that of the factory-worker, an artist forced to sell his skill to satisfy the conventional and vulgar demands of the market. What aggravated the situation even fur-ther was Norwid's "Polishness," which cut him off from the ma-jority of French society both for linguistic and cultural reasons; but, this "Polishness" was not conventional enough for his com-patriots, the only people who could have supported him, to war-rant much sympathy or enthusiasm. After the publication of his two long works *Promethidion* and *Zwolon,* the average literate Pole, whether in Paris or Poznań, was puzzled by Norwid's work and was unwilling to give financial or moral support for the pub-lication of such "rhymed nonsense." Norwid's isolation in Paris was then twofold: his native tongue and basically Polish ambi-tions isolated him from the French, while his enigmatic style and uncompromising artistic integrity isolated him from the Polish intellectual elite.

Nonetheless, settling down in Paris proved profitable for the poet on other counts. Here Norwid came to know and appreciate Mickiewicz more than before; he visited Słowacki and Chopin, met Hoene-Wroński and other distinguished Poles of the Great Emigration, and made the personal acquaintance of the great French historian Michelet. In Emma Herwegh's salon he met Alexander Herzen and Ivan Turgenev and, probably thanks to the mediation of Edmund Chojecki, an editor of *La Tribune des Peuples,* he became better acquainted with the theories and the personalities of the intellectual Left. Yet perhaps the most im-portant outcome of his stay in Paris was a direct confrontation with history. Revolution was followed by counterrevolution, a period of free and often chaotic debate was superseded by auto-cratic rule; not only ideas but social forces clashed violently in front of the poet's eyes. In this whirlpool of historical change Norwid managed to steer his mind toward philosophical and his-toriosophic conclusions: "There is a whiff of the declining Rome here" he wrote from Paris soon after Louis Napoleon's coup in 1851, ". . . the emperor tries his *fortune*—the rhetors are exiled, for the papers are closed down. As for us pale-faced émigrés, we are like the Nazarenes who know what will happen in a thousand

Promethidion

years time, but all that is within their reach is enchanted and
inaccessible. . . ." [1] Whatever political hopes he had attached to
the revolutionary upsurge of 1848–1849, by 1851 Norwid was in-
tensely skeptical about political programs and short-term solutions. He turned to philosophy and art theory. The result was
Promethidion.

II   Promethidion: *Bogumił*

Promethidion is a very ambitious undertaking. In this versed
poetic treatise in two dialogues with an epilogue, Norwid tried
to pose *and* answer all the esthetic and broadly philosophical
questions which he thought were relevant to most educated Poles
of the nineteenth century. In its form the poem resembles the
Platonic dialogues, and the nature of the discussion between
Norwid's protagonists, the challengers or mouthpieces of his
ideas, shows the author's familiarity with not only the Platonic
but also the Neoplatonic schools of esthetics. Winckelmann, the
great German art critic who rediscovered Greek art for his contemporaries, was another, rather obvious influence. Some critics
pointed out borrowings from, or parallels with, the esthetic theories of Lamennais and the Polish philosopher and reformer
Libelt.[2] The whole work, nevertheless, blends these different
influences in such a way as to create the impression of novelty
and originality.

The very title of the epic poem is a neologism coined from the
name of Prometheus and the Greek suffix *eidon*, meaning "the
son" or descendant of Prometheus. Prometheus, who presented
mankind with fire, is an archetypal figure from Hesiod and
Aeschylus onwards. He was interpreted by such different writers
as Goethe, Shelley, and Victor Hugo, and for the Romantics he
symbolized a satanic-humanist revolt against tyranny. He was
seen as an un-Christian teacher and savior of mankind. Polish
critics emphasized that Norwid was obviously more attracted to
Aeschylus's interpretation than that of Shelley; [3] others pointed
to Michelet's interest in the myth of Prometheus as a possible
influence on Norwid. It seems to me that Norwid's models should
be sought elsewhere. His ambition in *Promethidion* was to discuss
universal problems from a Polish angle. It is therefore not impossible that the title originates from the striking lines of Słowacki's *Agamemnon's Grave:*

Poland! . . .
. . . you are the only son of Prometheus:
But the vulture devours not your heart—your brains.[4]

Yet the key to Norwid's general and in some ways un-Romantic concept of *Promethidion* lies in the *Palingénésie* of the French philosopher P. S. Ballanche, whose work (and this can, and perhaps will, be proved by further research) exerted an overriding influence on Norwid's thought and work. Ballanche mentioned the name of Prometheus more than once in his long and seminal philosophical treatise, characterizing the hero of the Greek myth at one point in the following manner: *"Prométhée c'est l'homme se faisant lui-même par l'énergie de sa pensée."* [5] Prometheus is the man who creates himself through the energy of his thought, and, Ballanche continues, the conflict symbolized in his myth is the eternal conflict between the general "laws of history" and man's "existential will." Norwid regarded man as master of his own destiny. For him man was not a lonely rebel against a tyrannical God, but rather a rebel against the indifferent determinism of nature, social routine and historical stagnation. Prometheus's act of *rebellion* was less important for Norwid than his act of *creation*—the gift of fire that he gave mankind, the gift of tools for work and self-expression. "Fire" here stands for "word," for according to Ballanche (and Norwid) Prometheus awakened mankind from its semidormant state and made it conscious of its supreme task: to reach God through self-perfection. It is this Prometheus, the speech-giver, the patron saint of arts, that captured Norwid's imagination.

Yet in the poetic treatise itself the original myth of Prometheus is not discussed. Most of the poem is devoted to arguments and monologues on the nature or, even more ambitiously, on the essence of art. The first dialogue titled *Bogumił* is about *form* or the notion of beauty; whereas the second titled *Wiesław* is concerned with *content*, which is in Norwid's view goodness—and both principles are united in the light of truth. Bogumił's dialogue opens with a discussion in a salon on the merits of Chopin's music. It soon becomes a controversy about the aims and correct definition of beauty. Someone expresses the flippant view that beautiful is what "pleases everybody," whereupon Maurycy, a participant of the debate, ripostes with words that could be Norwid's own: "*Beautiful* is not . . . what *pleases* people at present or had pleased them in the past / *But what ought to please . . . what improves*" [6] (italics in the original). Beauty is not and cannot be the privilege of a caste or the leisured few, but there is something aristocratic in it and therefore not everyone can grasp beauty immediately. A Count declares that for him "order is beauty." This class-motivated view is challenged by Ambrozy, another member of the group. Subsequently, Bogumił, the main character of this part of *Promethidion*, expresses his view in an inspired monologue. He calls upon "the eternal man" to define the essence of beauty, uncontaminated by sectarian or political interests, independent of the whims of fashion. The answer is: beauty is "the Form of Love." Every person has the capacity to partake in this divine gift, either as a creator of things of beauty or as a recipient.

Between beauty and work there is a close connection. Bogumił, or rather his "Eternal Man," connects the two in a passage vital to Norwid's esthetic theory and quoted in most commentaries on this subject:

> Because beauty exists—to enchant
> and rouse to work—and work: to bring resurrection [7]

Bogumil-Norwid's interest in beauty is not confined to esthetics: it has an ethical aspect as well. The upper classes tend to subjectivize beauty, to equate it with the comfortably integrated, the convenient. This "subjectivism," argues Norwid, is a distortion of truth and leads, among other things, to social upheavals which then restore the "objective" meaning of beauty. As for the poet and the artist who creates beauty, he is also serving his community. This is the link between Bogumił's "ethical" interpretation of beauty and the statement that "the greatest poet is the simple people." Almost a Romantic-populist commonplace, it nevertheless reflects Norwid's admiration for popular art and folk-poetry, for he believed that genuine national art should arise and evolve from folk-art. This did not mean an imitation of folk-art *forms* (in which many lesser Romantics, including Lenartowicz, did indulge) but an openness to the inspiration of the people, an absorption of elements such as those that enriched Chopin's music. Folk-art should not be imitated but elevated to the level of high art. Here lies a striking similarity between Norwid's and Libelt's views, the latter writing in his *Aesthetics:* "The best example of how to create great art from folk-motifs was given to us by Chopin in his music." [8]

Bogumił's monologue ends with a detailed exposé of his concept of "national art." In Norwid's opinion Poland has not yet found its "form," its true artistic self-expression. Artistic taste is underdeveloped; the fine arts are hardly appreciated. Artists in Poland are martyrs: art "grows out of their ashes"—a theme which often recurs in Norwid's correspondence in later years. Now he dreams of something genuine and organic, a great "national chapel" growing out of the combined efforts of Polish artists—a feat of architecture in which the "Polish soul" would express itself. This vision, incidentally, shows that Norwid at this period was still more interested in painting than in literature. From this fragment of *Promethidion* it appears that he still regards fine arts as the highest form of artistic expression. But the art-theoretician changes into an apostle of future art in the often quoted passage that connects the fundamental (for Norwid) ideas of art and work: "And I see art in the Poland of the future/ As a *banner at the tower of human works* / Neither as a plaything nor as a kind of *science* / But like *the highest craft of an apostle* / And *the humblest prayer of an angel.*" [9]

Work has a double meaning and function for Norwid. Although he accepts the traditional Catholic idea that work is God's punishment inflicted on mankind for "the loss of Eden," he also believes that it is a means, if not *the* means, to human self-emancipation, in man's (Adam's) Promethean effort to reach God. Man's gradual perfection, on the other hand, is impossible without the humanization, or without a more Norwidian concept of the "spiritualization," of labor. Norwid is convinced that "unnecessary work has to vanish" and in fact will vanish, though not entirely, due to mechanization. He puts his faith into the possibility that "work [will be] *increasingly lightened by love,*" [10] for neither unbounded technological progress nor radical social reforms can change the basic nature of work which for Norwid is expiation.

This view involved more love than economic investment—a somewhat unrealistic program for 1851. But Norwid is aware of this: in a lengthy footnote he discusses the Great Industrial Exhibition just held in London in that year, expressing the hope that with this huge show of industrial might "industrial idolatry will reach its apogee" and a new kind of practical estheticism will develop. The main problem is that work is alienated from creativity, the artifact is merely useful, instead of satisfying man's innate sense of beauty. Norwid reflects upon this in the work's prose *Epilogue* which is a collection of thoughts and comments loosely connected with the treatise itself. The gap between beauty and usefulness can be bridged, he argues, through "the circulation of the idea of beauty"—not only should art be a continuation and triumphant culmination of work, but products of work should also be permeated by beauty through the production of esthetically pleasing artifacts. In Part XVIII of the *Epilogue* Norwid deplores the rigid barrier separating art galleries from industrial exhibitions: they should, ideally, constitute one organic entity! This is a modern idea which shows Norwid's foresight and affinity with such antiindustrial reformers as Ruskin and Morris. Jan Piechocki points out in his comparative study,[11] as regards their views on the nature of art and its connection with crafts—and let us add in many other respects—Ruskin and Norwid were thinking along similar lines. (An interesting comparison could be drawn between Ruskin's views on the undesirability of "perfection" as put forward in the *Stones of Venice* and on Norwid's later theories on the necessity of unfulfillment or *niedopełnienie*.) But while Ruskin's motives in revolting against the unimaginative taste of the age were, at least initially, purely esthetic, Norwid's esthetic views were inseparable from his philosophy and also from his social and patriotic attitudes. Most of these were expounded in the second half of *Promethidion* in the so-called Dialogue of Wiesław.

III   Promethidion: *Wiesław*

Whereas the first dialogue is mainly about art, the second one concentrates on a search to define truth. Wiesław, the main protagonist, describes the evolution of public opinion as the evolution of "mankind's conscience." The more man is permeated by conscience, the closer is he to God. Konstanty, another partner in the dialogue, calls this "mysticism, Schelling or Plato." Wiesław retorts with a somewhat cryptic remark about the nature of "mysticism," Norwid adding in a footnote that some people explain everything that is *beyond* reason as unreasonable; rejecting "mysticism" out of hand is plain superficiality or lack of humility toward things not yet understood.[12] This is, by the way, an unveiled criticism of Positivism; but some following passages indicate that Norwid's hero is also at odds with the Romantics.

To be sure, he acknowledges the legitimacy of the "prophetic mission": the true prophet has to fulfill two conditions only—to believe in the God of his Fathers and to fight *"for truth by truth"* (an implicit rejection of "Wallenrodism," a form of Romantic nihilism maintaining that a ruthless enemy may be fought with unethical methods based on Mickiewicz's poem *Konrad Wallenrod*). Furthermore, the prophet has to be disinterested and prepared to speak the truth *for its own sake*, not in the service of a cause however sublime. While the prophet is preoccupied with truth, the bard (*wieszcz*) fixes his sight on beauty. Both see only one side of the Essence and so they complement each other, neither of them having a monopoly of revelation. Poland also has its share of prophets, but autocracy and "stupidity" stifles their voice; their place is taken by politicians, charlatans and "fortune-tellers," for whom Norwid has but little respect. They represent only the superficial "outward" truth of the historical situation; they are play acting in mouthing ultranationalistic, ultraspiritual or simply loyalistic "truths," which are in fact self-justifications. Norwid is convinced that as long as people refuse to internalize truth, the resurrection of independent Poland is impossible; it will not happen before "Poland wins *the war of truth* with herself." [13] Prophetic words, recalling Słowacki at his most pessimistic. Truthfulness is more essential than will power and determination to defeat the enemy.

Some of the ideas expressed in a more or less elliptic fashion appear in the prose *Epilogue* once again. Each nation has its own particular contribution to the development of art. The starting point in the development of new Polish art is, symbolically, "Chopin's grave." Here the argument of the "Bogumił dialogue" is reiterated: through an internal evolution of the spirit the "popular" (*ludowy*) element could be elevated to the level of the "universal." In this the task of the Polish artist is enormous since "he has *to organize the national imagination*" in the same way as the statesman organizes the political forces of the nation. Norwid's ideal is clearly a healthy and organic society, which lives in harmony, honors its critics, and listens to its prophets. Yet he feels that there is a terrifying gap between the patriarchal, agrarian past and the free, industrial but esthetically organized future—especially in the case of Poland where the gap between the desperately poor peasant tilling the land and the property-owning classes is almost unbridgeable. While he does not advocate any concrete plan of reform in the *Epilogue* to *Promethidion,* his real, overriding concern is to rechannel Polish thinking into new categories. Instead of directing most attention to such "outward" problems as diplomatic or political ways and means of liberating Poland, he stresses the necessity of a greater "turning inwards," national self-analysis, and organic social work in the spirit of complete truthfulness. He is among the first Polish writers to defy "martyrology": *"the victory over one's own nation* . . . should lead to making martyrdom unnecessary: and that is PROGRESS"[14] (original emphasis retained). This last sentence sums up Norwid's rejection of Wallenrodian Romanticism, the ideology of exalted self-sacrifice that had mesmerized a whole generation since 1830–1831. For the author of *Promethidion,* a nation exists only inasmuch as it is conscious of its own problems. Without a dialogue between the constituent parts of the nation (what Norwid calls the "word of the people" and "the written word") no such consciousness can arise. The answer is work in the spirit of love; work, instead of armed insurrections, and the development of an art which is capable of "ennobling" and harmonizing Polish society into a single entity. The Norwid of *Promethidion* eschewed political action. After the revolutionary twilight of 1849–1851, he is disillusioned with politics and states with axiomatic brevity in the *Epilogue*: "Only to art, perceived in its full truth and dignity, can a Pole today devote his life."[15] Note the word "devote." From now on Norwid regards his creative work as a service not only to Poland but to mankind. He appears alternately in two roles—as philosopher unraveling the secrets of the past and as prophet foretelling the doom of the industrial civilization built on "money and blood."

IV *Evaluation*

While the immediate reception of *Promethidion* was very disappointing for the author (contemporary critics deplored its "obscurity," "forced mysticism," and his "unfortunate neologisms"), a few rare sympathetic readers such as J. B. Zaleski, a fellow-poet, noticed "the richness of its intelligence and of its language." The real renaissance of Norwid's poetic treatise came much later—after 1918 when it became a basic text in intellectual circles. It was recognized that some of his esthetic and social propositions formulated in an axiomatic and very quotable manner retained their relevance even in the first half of the twentieth century. The critics' praise was, however, not unqualified: "It is not merely a rhymed treatise . . . for it is interspersed with magnificent poetic visions. The larger part, however, undoubtedly possesses a didactic character with many obscure and difficult points." [16] What makes the enjoyment of *Promethidion* as poetry difficult is not so much its didactic character but its heterogeneity. The language of the poem oscillates between the discursive prose of the salon and a philosophically inclined lyrical rhapsody. Along with striking *poetic* formulations of ideas or impressive metaphors, there are thickets of lines puzzling in their deliberate (though perhaps only seeming) impenetrability. In other words, while *Promethidion* is a challenge to the explorer of Norwid's thought, one is left with the feeling that he has not yet found the golden mean between discreet didacticism and imaginative allusiveness which characterizes some of his best lyrics, especially the bulk of the *Vade-Mecum* cycle. *Promethidion* is an experimental piece of poetry. While parts of it stand by themselves as good pieces of descriptive or lyrical verse, the work as a whole is so obviously organized around the exposition of certain esthetic and ethical values that it is almost impossible to judge it from a purely literary viewpoint. One of Norwid's most sensitive critics, Tadeusz Makowiecki, sees the significance of this work precisely in terms of its ideas. As Norwid was the first Polish poet to realize that the Romantic Era had come to an end, he made a special effort to create a "synthetic antithesis": a kind of realism which does not reject Romanticism in its entirety but rather transcends it, while incorporating certain elements of the Romantic consciousness.[17] *Promethidion* is the result of this effort, and it is important and valuable in spite of its minor shortcomings.

CHAPTER 3

The Lyric Poet

I *The Short Poems: A Classification*

NORWID'S lyric poetry, or at least the bulk of it, was "occasional" in the sense that he often reacted to external events by writing poems about them. Vividly interested in social, historical, and philosophical problems he would not view human destiny in a vacuum but saw it in relation to the past as well as the future. Though purely philosophical reflections can also be found in Norwid's lyrical *oeuvre*, as a rule his imagination was set into motion by some particular event of historical or personal significance. In a sense, Norwid continued the Romantic tradition; like Słowacki, he would write lyric poems about a heroic gesture, the funeral of a well-known or a less known but noble hero, or an event that affected the life of Poles in or outside Poland. As with Słowacki the poem might well have been the by-product of his work on an epic poem or a play. The exception to this rule is *Vade-Mecum*, the great lyric cycle, which had been planned by the poet for years before realization. The cycle can be read as a general social and personal commentary on Norwid's age. Prior to *Vade-Mecum* Norwid seemed to attribute little importance to his lyrics. He often sent them, without making a copy of the original manuscript, to friends and indifferent editors; many of these lyrics were lost or remained unpublished until after the poet's death. Paradoxically, Norwid's epic works, such as *Quidam*, to which he attached great importance are read nowadays much less than the shorter, more emotional and more striking lyrics.

Norwid's lyric poems can be divided into four groups according to their poetic approach and subject matter. Polish readers know best the "heroic" poems, such as *The Funeral Rhapsody in Bem's Memory*, *To Citizen John Brown* and *Chopin's Piano*. These poems were written about outstanding personalities, heroes of a cause near to the poet's heart. They also were reactions to events which for Norwid symbolized important historical changes —the beginning or the end of an epoch, a turning point or (as in *Chopin's Piano*) the lowest point in the spiritual decline of a civilization. Although their pathos is no longer as direct and simple as in similar poems by Mickiewicz and Słowacki, they affect the reader's imagination in a "Romantic" way and point to Norwid's allegiance to the widely held article of faith of "universal freedom," a noble leftover from the pre-1849 period. Another difference between the patriotic poems of the great Romantics and the poems of Norwid discussed above lies in the fact that the latter's method is not descriptive but integrationalist, blending his esthetic views and philosophy of history into a vision transcending the event that serves as a starting point for the poem.

The second group comprises the "social" poems. In these, Norwid, as a keen observer of the social scene both in the East and the West (the conventions of Polish émigrés reflecting the conventions of Polish society), looks at the values and everyday conduct of his contemporaries relating them to the laws given to mankind by God—through Christianity—and to the ideals toward which mankind should strive. Here the poet's approach to the central problem posited in the poem can be "subjective" or "objective." He may or may not speak in the first person, but the subject matter is usually rooted in the social conditions of the age and is expressed through a symbol or a set of symbols. In the "social" poems Norwid's irony plays an important role; more often than not Norwid's attacks on the false conventions or smug hypocrisy of society are camouflaged by oblique statements, by ironical turns of speech, or in some cases, they are expressed in a line cut short of its conclusion. Although many of these poems, especially those of the *Vade-Mecum*, are widely known and often quoted, e.g., *Ghosts, Marionettes, Nerves* (*Larwa, Marionetki, Nerwy*), the full appreciation of quite a few of them is unusually difficult. Norwid often makes use of a certain kind of "elliptic speech" which—especially when sprinkled with neologisms and mysterious allusions—confused and irritated his contemporaries who were used to the smooth flow of Romantic poetry. Even today these features make the interpretation of these texts a matter of conjecture. In such cases the emphasis of a word or the position of a comma or a dash may be very important and the less patient reader just could not be bothered with guessing the meaning of a line that "did not speak for itself." Nonetheless, these "social" poems are central to Norwid's work, for they demonstrate his obsessive striving for truth in an age given to appearances, as well as his ethically motivated historicism, so relevant to our own reality. His deep-cutting and embittered criticism of nineteenth-century industrial society meant a self-definition in face of the then prevailing conditions and conventions, a chance to expound his own view of human history. His negation of what he considered antihuman contained a positive and evolutionary program for the future.

Into the third category fall those poems which could be broadly defined as "private." As regards love-poems Norwid was one of the most reserved Polish poets of the age. He wrote very few poems which revealed his feelings toward or about women and most of those were written in his youth. It would be wrong, however, to think that Norwid was immune to the temptations of the fair sex. While his unfortunate romance with Maria Kalergis was well-known and probably much ridiculed in Polish émigré circles, it can be safely assumed that he had interest in other women; for instance, probably something more than a Platonic friendship bound him to Zofia Węgierska. Yet he never referred directly to the beloved person by name in his poems, and his shyness and an exaggerated sense of honor and loyalty were reflected in the discreet tone and allusiveness of his most "private" verse. From this it can be deduced that he never had a normal love life; as Błoński rightly observed in his excellent study, Norwid literally "exiled himself from love" because of his high demands *vis-à-vis* women.[1] There is an inherent duality in all the female characters appearing in his poems or dramas reflecting a contradiction between Norwid's ideal, which is closer to the early Christian than to the Second Empire type of women or the middle- or upper-class women he met throughout his life. It might be significant that only in one epic poem (*Assunta*) was Norwid able to create a woman who, while embodying some of the supreme Christian virtues, lived in the nineteenth century. The price of this unique combination was the heroine's inability to speak.

Some of the "private" poems, (in the form of poetic letters) were written to friends with whom Norwid was corresponding or addressed to people who made a lasting impression on him (*To a Famous Russian Dancer, Sonnet to Marcel Guyski*). Although in the "social" poems Norwid tended to avoid the first person singular thus trying to desubjectivize his poetic statement, in the "private" poems he uses this device rather frequently, which lends the poem an air of poetic confession. Poems like *Whether I'll ask for amnesty?* (1856) and *To My Contemporaries* (1867) are good examples of this genre. In the first the poet describes the desperate predicament which forced him to emigrate to the United States rather than return to Poland, and goes on to explain why it is impossible for him to return to his homeland *now* (after the Crimean War), when the Tsar made a few minor concessions including an amnesty for Polish political refugees. This is a poem based on a very subjective, emotional argument which rings true. The second poem, though it begins with a metaphor not unlike the first ("And I said farewell to my land and pushed away / with my feet the familiar shores. . . ."), continues with a bitter criticism of Polish provincialism and political short-sightedness, only to return in the last stanza to a personal problem of Norwid's, namely, the obscurity of his style. While the poetic framework is very personal, the axiomatic formulation of the poet's criticism of Polish society at the end of the first stanza sounds very much like a quote from a "social" poem:

A country! where every deed comes too early
But—every book . . . too late! [2]

The fourth group comprises epigrams and poems of the *fraszka* type which range from the mildly satirical to bitterly ironic pieces. Most of these poems could be classified as "social" in their aspirations or criticisms, though their briefness predestined them to become more of a convenient vehicle of Norwid's political ideas rather than his broader views on society, a corollary to his religious and historiosophic ideas. Norwid jotted down about half a dozen such short poems in the period between 1849 and 1852 when he was working on more ambitious projects such as *Promethidion* or the mystery plays. Of these epigrams one or two have remained topical until our days; for example, *Fraszka (!)* I, with its intransigent Polish "patriots" locked in a fierce argument over the political form of a liberated Poland of the future, but agreeing that the terrible status quo is preferable to the victory of the rival's political system. Another gem is *Their Strength* (*Siła ich*), an ironic survey of the forces of tyranny in the mid-nineteeth and, alas, also in the twentieth century which deserves quotation in full:

> Vast armies, valiant generals, police
> Of either sex, secret or seen, what can
> It be that so unites their prejudice?
> Just a few thoughts—and these as old as man.[3]
> (English version by Christine Brooke-Rose)

II   The People's Hands were Swollen

There are, of course, quite a few poems by Norwid which cannot be put squarely into any of these groups, since they blend and unite elements of each, being "heroic," "social," "private," and even "epigrammatic" in turn. Such a poem is *Klaskaniem mając obrzękłe prawice . . .* (quoting the first line of this untitled poem): *The People's Hands Were Swollen with Applause,* which is a grand poetic summary of its author's struggles, frustrations and hopes. The approach is confessional and autobiographical—indeed, almost any line could be used in a monograph for a motto of some period in Norwid's life. It was written in 1858, but Norwid placed it with the *Vade-Mecum* cycle completed only by 1865. The significance attributed to this poem by its author makes it a good target for a closer textual analysis. The following quotations are from Christine Brooke-Rose's English version.

The People's Hands . . . opens with a dramatic but at the same time ironic description of the situation prevailing in Polish poetry before Norwid's appearance:

> The people's hands were swollen with applause,
> But they were bored by poetry and cried
> For deeds . . .[4]

which, read together with the next line or two, including the phrase "handsome laurels sighed," while showing the political situation in partitioned Poland (people have no freedom, only poetry as a kind of freedom-substitute) already defines Norwid's stand toward the great Romantics, Mickiewicz, Krasiński and to a much lesser extent toward Słowacki. "The people cried for deeds" is an allusion to the revolutionary ferment growing in all parts of former Polish territories between 1842 and 1848; it also reflects the influence of Cieszkowski's philosophy, especially his critique of Hegel and his special emphasis on action. "And it was laurel-dark in my country" the English version goes on, whereas Norwid says: *laurowo i ciemno*—"the country was full of laurels and it was dark." Thus, reverence for poetry went together with futile heroic gestures and with political ignorance. It was out of this land of tragic darkness that God called Norwid—like his prophets or apostles—and bade him live "in life's wilderness" (*w żywota pustyni*)—in the loneliness of exile.

The first two stanzas are in fact the poet's self-definition in relation to his country and to his great predecessors, though in the second stanza Norwid states, more in defiance than in sorrow, that he does not owe anything to those "giants" of poetry whose work had sustained the Polish nation since the lost war of independence of 1830–31. He does not share fame ("laurels") with the great Romantics; he has followed their trails but found only decay and destruction. This statement is perhaps less important than the last line of the second stanza: "I came alone, I wander on, alone." He is not only independent of even the greatest poets of the previous epoch, but his separateness is total, his poetic road is unique. Norwid did not belong to the first generation of the Great Emigration; he came too late to benefit from Western sympathy for the Poles, but at the same time (this is clear from the conclusion of the poem) he believed that he had come too early for his age. Originality, of course, has its own risks; in the line quoted above Norwid uses the verb *błądzić*, which can be translated as "to wander on," but means rather something like "to stray," "to blunder." There are no well-trodden footpaths for the original artist—he has to cut his own path in the forest, even if this entails the risk of going astray.

This poetic journey continues in the next stanza. Here Norwid comes closest to social criticism in the poem, and it is the ingrained traditionalist, the tooth-and-nail conservative who gets his worst strictures: "I have met many turned towards a past / Unfathomable yet worshipped still; / My heel has knocked on spurs engrained with rust, / All along paths where many a bullet fell." The poet is suggesting here that the admirer of the past does not necessarily understand the past, and that certain institutions or privileges which may have served a purpose at one time can become obstacles of human progress a few decades later. While Norwid often clashed with radical opinion and went on record several times (for instance during the Paris Commune) to denounce the extremists of the Left, it is remarkable that in his lifetime he got the worst blows and the least appreciation from his conservative critics, from the enraged traditionalists of Poznań and Cracow. Those who did not want "to break with dreams" ridiculed Norwid's program of national rebirth suggested in the *Promethidion;* subsequently they did not even bother to listen to what Norwid was saying because he said it in such a peculiar way, wrapping up his message in parables, difficult allusions, or symbols.

The fourth stanza informs us of the gap between the ideal and reality as regards women. The hypocrisy and inertia of Polish society appears in its purest form in the behavior of women who are "enchanted in dead formulas"—a phrase quoted earlier in connection with the Kalergis affair. Since Norwid believed that Maria Kalergis failed to reciprocate his love mainly because of her own ambitions and the incompatibility of their social status, he concluded that slavish adherence to convention made "the marble lady" unattainable. Yet Norwid must have had other experiences that confirmed his negative view of the ladies of high society (he speaks about "a thousand . . . such females") whose real home is the salon and whose caprices, airs, and pretensions alienate the man who is looking for a real partner, not a dressed-up doll whom he can adore.[5] Failure in love makes happiness seem "inconceivable." After this confession the poem plunges to its nadir of despair where the "Sunday of satiation," the image of the age, is contrasted with the penury and sorrow of the lonely poet who finally throws into the face of this society his last word of contempt: "I ask for nothing—*executioners!*"

Executioners? The word should be interpreted here in a nonphysical sense. The callousness, the mad drive of this society after money, its sheer insensitivity and incomprehension killed the poet's natural belief in his fellowmen, slaughtered his ambitions and showed that with strong moral inhibitions one can hardly escape complete starvation. If my reading is correct, the exclamation "executioners!" is not directed against an unrespon-

sive public or against middle-class women, themselves products
of a certain social milieu, but it is the condemnation of crass
bourgeois morals of the age when "*enrichissez-vous!*" could be
a generally accepted imperative regardless of the consequences.
While industrialists and entrepeneurs gobble up huge profits, the
impoverished intellectual stands apart, observing the scene with
stoic contempt. As for the poet: "I write—well, sometimes— *to
Jerusalem / Via Babylon . . .*," which is to say from the corrupted
present to the cleansed future, or else—another possible interpretation—from and "through" Paris to an ideal, liberated Warsaw.
Whether he is right or wrong in what he is doing, he cannot say,
only time will tell—his subjective justification being that he is
writing "the memoirs of an artist." This work may well be rejected by society as "mad," but no one can doubt its "reality."
This genuineness separates, almost isolates Norwid from the illusions and "unreality" of the age, from the political slumber of
the masses and the indifference of the ruling classes. In his lectures on Słowacki, Norwid spoke about two kinds of contemporaneity; in the same way he believed that there are two kinds
of reality and that his inner reality is deeper and more lasting
than the ephemeral reality of the outside world.

The poem ends with a prophecy; Norwid, not unlike Byron in
Canto IV of *Childe Harold,* foresees the inevitable triumph of
his art, his posthumous victory:

> The son will pass this writing by, but his son
> Will recall what vanishes to-day (now read
> In haste) under the rule of Print-Pantheism,
> Under the administration of the lead
> Letter. As it was in the forbidden
> Catacombs below Rome's sunny clay,
> Where realness struts in error, unastonished,
> So he will re-read what you read to-day,
> And will recall me, since I will have vanished.[6]

The People's Hands . . . is one of the longest poems in the
Vade-Mecum cycle, and its formal structure is unusually rich and
varied. Each stanza has a different rhyme scheme with the exception of stanzas two and four, which have a consistent *abab-
cdcd* pattern. Each line is rhymed (some of the rhymes are
strinkingly unusual) and consists of eleven syllables, a rather

popular line in nineteenth-century Polish poetry. The poem's main forte lies in its vivid imagery and the successful fusion of emotion and thought which is characteristic of Norwid's best work. Even if certain metaphors show Słowacki's influence or an affinity with Słowacki's imagery,[7] the vocabulary of the poem is highly idiosyncratic. Archaic words and expressions occur next to newly coined compound words or neologisms (Sunday of satiation, Print-Pantheism), while some words carry a heavy load of subjective meaning (*rzeczywisty*—real). All this makes the poem more difficult to grasp and interpret at first reading, but it is undoubtedly one of the key poems to Norwid's whole *oeuvre*, a poem which even now, more than a hundred years after it was written, retains its force and topicality.

III Vade-Mecum

During the fifteen years following the publication of *Promethidion* Norwid wrote about a hundred and thirty lyric poems. His most popular and most often quoted poems were set down on paper at this time, poems such as *The Funeral Rhapsody in Bem's Memory, To Citizen John Brown, Spartacus, Three Strophes,* and the famous *Chopin's Piano.* This was a period full of change both in Norwid's personal life and in the life of the Polish emigration. Norwid, penniless and with a broken heart, emigrated to the United States only to return two years later, spurred on by the news of the Crimean War. Mickiewicz died, and a few years later Krasiński passed away as well. Norwid gave public lectures on Słowacki and achieved a new reputation in the eyes of a few fellow-countrymen; and he lived through the rise of national hopes which were shattered once again with the failure of the the uprising of 1863. From the point of view of the poet, however, the entire period constituted a time of gestation for *Vade-Mecum.*

According to Norwid's most knowledgeable living critic and editor J. W. Gomulicki [8] Norwid began the consistent formulation of his poetic program around 1859. The word "poetic" should be emphasized, for in *Promethidion* Norwid had already defined his social and esthetic views; but while Mickiewicz and Krasiński were still alive, Norwid's authority to formulate a poetic program transcending the achievements of Polish Romanticism was not established. By the early 1860's this situation had changed· the "architect" (Krasiński), the "sculptor" (Mickiewicz) and the "painter" (Słowacki) of Polish poetry were all dead.[9] The time of the "artist-philosopher" had come. Standing alone on the ruins of Romanticism. Norwid knew that from now on he had no real rivals. He wrote to Kraszewski in 1866: "Polish poetry will go where the main part of *Vade-Mecum* is pointing with its meaning, meter, rhythm and example. Do they want it or not? it is all the same." [10]

The kind of lyric poetry that forms the bulk of *Vade-Mecum* was defined by Norwid as "poetry of history" as distinct from the "poetry of nature" cultivated by most of his contemporaries writing in Polish. The latter category included descriptive nature poems, love poems, poems on historical figures or events, and Romantic ballads displaying a wealth of passion and emotion. As his remarks about Słowacki's *Balladyna* show, Norwid never denied the value of such poetry but had higher regard for "the poetry of history" and maintained that one of the chief weaknesses of Polish poetry was the lack of "moralistic" verse. *Vade-Mecum* put forward a new set of poetic propositions. These poems born out of moral convictions and sound intellectual judgment were contemplative, basically nondescriptive, and not merely emotional; they were meant to reflect not only the surface but the deeper, invisible reality of the age. The poet's convictions that informed these poems were part of a larger, historiosophic vision. Throughout the cycle Norwid was engaged in a search for that "deeper contemporaneity" referred to in the Słowacki lectures which, as it were, coexists with the shallow contemporaneity of everyday life. What made the cycle a lasting poetic achievement was not, of course, just Norwid's sincerity or truthfulness but also the means by which he questioned and challenged contemporary reality and by which he postulated a future more sympathetic to his own mode of thinking.

Vade-Mecum, never printed as a separate entity during the poet's lifetime, originally consisted of one hundred poems with an introductory poem, *Truisms*, and *To Valentine Pomian Z.* added to the cycle as an epilogue. This fact and some other structural and thematic similarities with Baudelaire's *Les Fleurs du Mal* (first published in 1857) prompted Gomulicki to state that *Vade-Mecum* was meant to be, in part, an "answer" to Baudelaire's famous book of verse.[11] While Norwid could have read Baudelaire's poems (he was certainly familiar with Baudelaire's

The Lyric Poet

art criticism, for he was interested in the fine arts and had friendly relations with more than one French painter), the contention that both *Vade-Mecum* and *Les Fleurs du Mal* are built around the same central antinomy, i.e., "ideal-reality," is far too general to prove anything except both artists' aversion to social reality. Also, whereas Norwid often hinted at his rivalry with, or dislike of, other Polish poets, he never tried to compete with his French contemporaries, and in his whole voluminous correspondence Baudelaire's name is not mentioned even once, whereas others, like Victor Hugo, are referred to repeatedly. Norwid and Baudelaire were contemporaries, lived in the same town, frequented similar social circles, and to a certain extent, were grappling with similar problems, such as the devaluation of Romantic ideals, the artist's alienation from industrial society ruled by money and permeated by philistine taste. Yet their answers and, more important, their respective attitudes to the age were entirely different. Nothing could be more repulsive to Norwid than Baudelaire's fake "satanism" and sterile narcissism. Would he acknowledge Baudelaire's cycle of poems as a real challenge to his poetry? It is very unlikely; rather, he regarded Baudelaire's art as just another symptom of the moral disease of the epoch.

It is questionable whether *Vade-Mecum*, had it reached the readers for whom it was intended soon after its completion, would have made a decisive impact on the further course of Polish poetry. Its didacticism—neither patriotic nor revolutionary—would have been resented and the poet's message only partly understood. Judging from the titles, the "eccentric" author of *Promethidion* was presenting here a rhymed handbook of philosophy and ethics: out of eighty-seven titles, sixty-one were nouns (four-fifths of them abstract); this, together with seven nouns preceded by adjectives, resulted in sixty-eight noun-centered titles. In the course of reading these poems, however, this "abstractness" gives way to genuine appreciation, for titles such as *Socialism, Hero,* or *Nerves* hide poetry rich in thought and feeling. As for didacticism, Norwid was certainly "incapable of turning a didactic intention into a biased argument or a compromised form." [12] His didacticism consists of using various poetic devices to reach simple truth through a complex dialectical method. This method has its drawbacks and occasionally leaves the reader bogged down in an obscure allusion, or leads him to a too neat definition dangerously close to a commonplace. Where it works, and it certainly works in the majority of the poems included in *Vade-Mecum*, we have thoughtful and gripping poems, comparable to the best of Emerson or Browning.

The innovations of *Vade-Mecum* are numerous. To begin with subject matter: life in the big town, in a metropolis, had never before been treated in Polish poetry with such realism and at the same time on such a high symbolic level. Mickiewicz treading the pavements of Paris was preoccupied with the noble past or with Poland's future; there is hardly any trace of the real Paris in his poetry. Norwid in poems like *Capital, Ghosts* (Polish title *Larwa*) or *Nerves* describes the complete loneliness of the individual in the faceless urban crowd, the monotony of industrial society, the misery of those who cannot accommodate to the rules of the game dictated by the Stock Exchange. There is no Romantic posturing in these poems, but the Positivists' enthusiasm for progress is absent as well; as for the subject matter, Norwid's "urban" poems could have been written thirty or forty years later, but they could have been equally well written by Blake. The anticapitalist, or simply the alienation-protest theme (for Norwid alienation was a symptom of materialism), appears in a highly compressed and symbolical form in the short poem *The Two Siberias*. Here Norwid shocks the reader with the statement that more than one Siberia exists: there is a geographically located Siberia under the frosty skies of Russia and another, a spiritual one, in the West—a frozen waste of "money and work" which exterminates freedom with an indifference equal to the physical Siberia. This metaphor has more than a subjective relevance; while it expresses the bitterness and frustration of the émigré artist, it also describes the life of the urban poor in France during the Second Empire. Recent research has established that during the Second Empire working-class poverty was much greater and much more widespread than had been thought; the French worker around 1860 worked longer and lived in worse conditions than his English counterpart.[13] The Paris Commune was not simply the outcome of a political crisis, since under Napoleon III middle-class living standards had improved at the cost of the proletariat. Norwid was not a Socialist and did not have to work eleven or twelve hours a day in a factory to eke out a living. But in a sense he was living on the margins of society, often on the verge of starvation, sharing and understanding the privations of the have-nots. He had very definite notions about the nature of work and believed that mechanical, unfree work humiliates the worker and robs him of his humanity. Such work is slavery, whether performed in Russia or in France. In the last stanza of *The Two Siberias* Norwid turns into a prophet of change; the Spirit (working through history) will one day demolish both kinds of slavery.

Another type of poem, common in *Vade-Mecum*, does not criticize society or social circumstances prevalent in society, but analyzes the meaning of certain notions. What is truth? What is the difference between "greatness" and greatness? What is progress? Time? What is man? These questions had never before been asked in Polish poetry so directly, and Norwid, asking them, was probing not only philosophy but also language, for his answers (determined by the nature of his genre) had to be more axiomatic than exact, had to be formulated in poetic rather than scientific terms. In *Sphinx (II)* the poet's truth about the human predicament is as follows: "*Man?—he is an ignorant and immature priest. . . .*" [14] In other words, in the "philosophical" poems of *Vade-Mecum* Norwid is giving poetic answers to ontological and existential questions and thereby stretches the language beyond its conventional poetic borders. Here the unusual subject matter often produces unusual solutions.

The novelty in Norwid's poetic technique lies in the dialectical method of verse construction, the main elements of which are allusiveness, irony, and the frequent use of symbols and intermissions. Certain critics emphasize the characteristic "fragmentariness" of Norwid's verse, its reliance on half-statements, pauses, and conscious omissions (*niedomówienia*). Of the factors listed above, irony is the most important. Norwid's poetry is permeated by irony which he uses to achieve a wide range of effects. He himself pointed out a difference between "historical" and "individual," or situational, irony. The irony of history is part of the world-order. In spite of all the human effort toward progress, the human race seems to be fighting a Sisyphean struggle as each generation fails to realize all its plans and thus, despite all the goodwill and hard work, society remains and continues to remain imperfect. The situation of a person who could have done much but is prevented by circumstances from doing his best for his community is also ironical. The mainspring of Norwid's irony is a feeling of incompleteness. To put it another way, it is human awareness of the difficulties and defeats that man suffers on his way to "resurrection." [15] The only way to fill the gap between ideal and reality is either by faith (projected into the future) or by irony (related to the present).

Irony has many different faces in *Vade-Mecum*. In one *fraszka* entitled *Mysticism* Norwid compares the mountaineer losing his way in the clouds of the Alps to the person who gets lost in mysticism; the fact that one *can* lose one's way in a cloud does not mean that the cloud (the mystic experience) does not exist. While this poem consists of questions and answers, and in fact ends with a question, another poem, *Vanitas*, is a series of short statements ranged together one after the other. Each statement asserts the superiority now of this, now of that nation, supporting this alleged superiority with suitable arguments: "The Minister of Enlightenment every year / tells the French that they are the cleverest; / the Englishman rates himself just as high / though the Italians won't stand comparison!" The irony increases in further stanzas, culminating in the claim of the Chinese in the fourth stanza that they are "the center of the world." Finally, all claims of competing nationalisms (including the Polish) are settled by the author in the last stanza where he states that it is impossible to tell truth from delusion until "opinions become more sincere" and people stop quarreling about national preeminence. In this poem irony is the simplest device by which the claims of contending and self-deluding nationalisms can be made to look ridiculous without making any direct counterstatement.

In the case of *Mysticism* and *Vanitas* irony is used to demonstrate the illogicality inherent in certain views or attitudes. There is another kind of irony which cuts both ways, that is, outward and against one's own self. This appears in situations where the poet is personally involved, for instance in *Nerves*. This is basically the description of two visits: a real one to a slum in Paris and another imaginary one to the salon of a certain Baroness. These two milieus clash in the poet's mind, as his own attitudes clash in his conscience. "They die of hunger in a certain place / where I went yesterday . . .": these opening lines are followed by the recollection of a near-accident in which the poet almost fell over the banister of an old staircase. When writing the poem he is still under the shock of his visit to the slums but already contemplating the next visit—to that most elegant salon. What can he say, how much can he communicate of the experience that upset him so much? For if he really speaks his mind

> The mirror will crack. The candelabra
> Will have convulsions at such *realism*.
> The painted parrots on the long macabre
> Ceiling beak to beak will shriek: *Socialism!*
>
> So—I shall take a seat, holding my hat
> In my hand, putting it down next to me . . .
> Then I shall return home—just like that—
> After the party—a dumb Pharisee.[16]
> (English version by Christine Brooke-Rose)

In the case of *Nerves* a typographical device, often used by Norwid, helps us in deciphering the hidden meaning of the poem. When he caught the beam in the staircase of the dilapidated building "where people die of hunger," Norwid noticed that a nail was stuck in it—"as on *the cross*". After the party, which he sat through without mentioning his experience, he returned home "a dumb Pharisee." On a higher, symbolical plane the sufferings witnessed in the slums, whether the person who died of starvation was an elderly worker or a pauperized émigré, were not different from Christ's sufferings on the cross. To keep silent about this is treason against Christ. On the other hand, social injustice of this kind is sanctioned by society and raising the matter in the salon would be useless. There is much irony in a situation in which speaking one's mind leads to social condemnation, while silence leads to a deep feeling of shame.

There is something very modern about *Nerves*. It is neither a Romantic protest nor is it a "social poem" in the naturalistic vein. While certain details are observed with the eye of a "microrealist" (e.g., the moldered beam in the staircase, the satin sofa of the Baroness), others, like the bold image of painted parrots shrieking in indignation, smack of Surrealism. The whole poem nevertheless is based on an interplay of symbols. Conceived in the spirit of *moral symbolism*, Norwid's symbolism precedes the French symbolist movement and is rather different from it. In Norwid's case the image is not autonomous, it is still subordinated to thought, in fact it is an agent of thought. Certain other poems of *Vade-Mecum* as well as earlier ones, such as *The Funeral Rhapsody in Bem's Memory*, show a conscious poetic design in the application and frequent use of symbols—the symbol as the secret sign of a "conspiracy" of ideas. (Here Norwid, an avid and sometimes unscholarly linguist, might have taken into account the original Greek meaning of the word *symbolos*—token, watchword, secret sign). Norwid's symbolism has to be seen against the background of his historiosophic and general esthetic concepts. Influenced by the ideas of the French philosopher and writer P. S. Ballanche, mentioned earlier, Norwid might have agreed with Ballanche's dictum: "Everything is a symbol." The thought itself is not new. It is simply a restatement of a belief held by many philosophers and poets, but in an epoch seeing the triumphant rise of materialism and positivism it did acquire new significance. If the world is perceived as a riddle which each person has to solve alone, if history and life are full of hidden meaning, then each fact, each event could be seen and interpreted as a symbol, a sign of something else, something invisible, unarticulated, not quite definable. Actions, gestures, nuances of speech can be symbolic, too.

In other words, Norwid, though not a mystic, was totally immersed in a lifelong search for "the hidden meaning" of the world. This explains his predilection for elliptic statements and parables, his high regard for Saint Paul and the ancient Greek philosophers, especially Plato. His attitude toward time and reality also derives from the same impulse. In his poetry he considers time in both its "linear" and "nonlinear" (eternal, symbolic) as pects [17] and divides reality into two categories, that of meaningful and that of purely factual reality. So the moral Symbolism of *Vade-Mecum* (very different from the pure Symbolism of a Mallarmé) posits eternal time and meaningful reality in place of actual historical time and superficial, material reality.

The fragmentariness of Norwid's poem-structures has been often bemoaned by critics as an obstacle to the understanding of his work. More recently Makowiecki and others have tried to direct critical attention to the philosophical background of Norwid's principle of *przemilczenie* (unsaying, concealment, leaving things unsaid). It is bound up with the problem of the "organic link," of cultural continuity. In this case, each sentence states something but each leaves something unsaid. The duty of the seeker after truth is "to perceive what has been left really unsaid in the last sentence, action or historical fact and to say, to add that [unsaid thing] moving the 'chain of truth' a link ahead." [18] While Norwid tried to "complete" what had been left unsaid by his great Romantic predecessors, he himself applied this technique to a considerable extent. Often in *Vade-Mecum* the poem does not end with a clear point, and if there is a moral, it is hidden in a riddle, a question, or in an ambiguous verbal structure. In one case the poem ends with the instruction: "guess it yourself!" (*Bliscy*). Why did Norwid use this technique which could only confirm the opinions and prejudices of those who claimed that his poetry was too "obscure" to be enjoyed? The answer lies in one of Norwid's basic assumptions about the nature of poetry: it is a dialogue between the poet and the reader. The latter is expected to cooperate with the poet in completing the poem, filling out the gaps which were left for him on purpose. Also, it can be assumed that in this respect Norwid was following the Socratic tradition in which the philosopher does not utter the truth, he only asks such questions as lead his partner to the truth; the reader is expected to complete the chain of logic.[19]

Norwid replied more than once to critics complaining about the "obscurity" of his texts. In a poem entitled *Obscurity* (Ciemność), which was included in *Vade-Mecum* but received its final form only in 1877, he connects the understanding of his work with the reader's faith in the validity of his truth. Those who do not make an effort to understand *his* quest for truth have never sought truth themselves but accepted the truisms of society: "Who complains of my obscure speech? / He who never lit himself a candle / but had a valet bring it to his room." [20] In a public lecture Norwid defined his priorities in the following manner: "The duty of the public speaker is *clearness in Truth*, not in the *letter* itself" and "Truth embraces life, so it is unclear, because it embraces a dark thing. . . ." [21] All the same, the obscurities in Norwid's work are not all due to the same cause. His poems abound in allusions grasped by some, but not all, contemporaries; they contain enigmatic lines which were formulated in this way in order to achieve an ambiguous effect; and finally, there must be cases of inadequacy, when the poet's neologism was unfortunate or choice of words clumsy, when the language was twisted too much to serve the poet's purpose. In *Vade-Mecum* on the whole (provided that one accepts Norwid's framework of thought and idiosyncratic ways of expression) no poems present an insurmountable difficulty in understanding, though many are understood better with accompanying notes. Generally speaking, as Norwid's "dark" lines have a functional relationship to the meaning of the whole text and that text can be related to the totality of his thought, it is easier to grasp them than the artful obscurities of a Mallarmé.

From a formal point of view *Vade-Mecum* did not bring anything dramatically new to Polish poetry, with the possible exception of the free verse used in *Chopin's Piano*. During the first decade after 1849 Norwid abandoned the eight-syllabic trochaic line, very popular among his contemporaries. Having departed from syllabotonic verse he used the eleven- or thirteen-syllable line most frequently, though in *Vade-Mecum* still another line, the ten-syllabic stressed line, dominates, with an inner caesura coming after the fourth syllable. This form (laconic in comparison to the thirteen-syllable line used, among others, in *Pan Tadeusz*), could have caught Norwid's attention when he was reading the translation of Serbian and Greek folk-ballads by Zaleski and Zmorski.[22] In general, *Vade-Mecum* is characterized by loose metric structures and by a conscious effort to make the poem less "ringing," more content-communicative, more prosaic. A variety of methods is used toward this end, including the interpolation of colloquial expressions in formal poetic speech, the frequent use of pauses and of special emphasis indicated by a different setting of the word or sentence to be emphasized. Sometimes these techniques appear simultaneously within the same stanza in which case the effect can be not so much prosaic as dramatic. It could be argued that the precondition of this heightened dramatic effect is precisely the depoetization of Romantic poetic speech—its break-up into statement, question, hint, and pause—and that Norwid was experimenting in *Vade-Mecum* with a new diction based on a less poetic but in some ways more expressive, elliptic, and intellectual language of his own.

IV   Chopin's Piano

Chopin's Piano (poem XCIX in *Vade-Mecum*) has an important place in Norwid's poetic *oeuvre*. It has been hailed as the
expression of Norwid's "most authentic lyricism" and as a "masterpiece of sound." While it has all the characteristic features of
a poem written by Norwid, in some respects it transcends the
still existing barrier which separates the author of *Vade-Mecum*
from popularity. Reasons for this should not be sought in the
simplicity of the poem: it is long and complex enough, but on
the other hand it displays many virtues which make it attractive
even for the uninitiated. These include a personal tone, a theme
close to the heart of admirers of Chopin's music (and indeed to
most Poles, proud of their internationally best known composer),
and a spirited combination of symbols with historical events
which finally elevates the poem to a universal plane, making the
fate of *Chopin's Piano* a concern for all.

Though the poem was written sometime around 1863 or 1864
and reached its final form about a year later, Norwid's admiration
for Chopin dated from much earlier. He made the composer's acquaintance in Paris and met him several times, including a visit
shortly before Chopin's death, which he alluded to in the opening lines of *Chopin's Piano:* "I was with you one of those last
days. . . ." His admiration for Chopin's music was apparent both
from *Promethidion* and from the obituary he wrote on Chopin's
death. In the obituary he exalted Chopin for his deep attachment
to his native country and stressed that although this outstanding
artist spent most of his life abroad he remained "a Pole in his
heart." Chopin's example showed that there was no inherent contradiction between Polishness and universality, that one could
attain perfection in conveying the message of one's native country to the world. In spite of his personal acquaintance with
Chopin, Norwid tended to regard him as a being of a higher
order, as the embodiment of all that is great and noble in Polish
culture.

Chopin's Piano contains 117 lines with ten stanzas of varying
length. The poem does not fit neatly into any known genre: in
some respects its a threnody, in others it is an ode, while Norwid
himself might have referred to it as a "rhapsody." Two main poetic threads run through the poem—the "Piastian-rural" and the

"Orphic." These threads might in fact correspond to the classical-romantic dichotomy certainly present but, according to Norwid, reconciled and harmonized in Chopin's achievement. The "Piastian" element [23] dominates in descriptions of Chopin's music, especially in the fifth stanza: "And in that music there was Poland / taken from the zenith of complete perfection in history / in a rainbow of ecstasy—/ the Poland—of the *transfigured wheelwrights!*" The explanation of the last phrase would warrant a lengthy exposition of Norwid's linguistic theories; here it suffices to say that he believed that Piast, the first Polish king, was the inventor of the wheel (*piasta* meaning a barrel in which the axis of the wheel is turning) and hence the creator of "social communication." The idealized and mythologized figure of the first Polish king stands for the golden age in Norwid's imagination. Still in the same stanza, the unusual phrase "golden beeful" *(złoto-pszczola),* while referring to the legendary kingdom of the Piasts evokes another age as well—that of sixteenth-century Poland, often called the "golden age" of Polish literature. This adjective evokes associations leading to Kochanowski, greatly admired by Norwid, who was the first Polish poet to praise the simple delights of the country, the perfect peace of mind that a man of clear conscience can enjoy among lime trees and humming bees. The golden age recalled by Chopin's music is distinctly rural.

Norwid's vision of ancient Poland and his admiration for classical beauty blend in the fourth stanza. Chopin's music is praised here for its "simplicity of Periclean perfection" which "as if some ancient Virtue / entering a larch-house in the village / were to say to itself: / 'I was reborn in heaven.' . . . ." Here the connection between the ancient virtue and "Periclean perfection" is clear; Periclean Athens, as well as Kochanowski's Poland, created an art of high esthetic value, a kind of classicism which, in Norwid's eyes, was inseparable from the moral standards of society.

At first glance, Stanza VII looks as if Norwid was trying to define Chopin's achievement in esthetic terms, but a closer reading reveals that he was really concerned with the impossibility of perfection in any work of art. Though Chopin's work contains much beauty and much truth ("Oh, You! who are the profile of Love / the name of which is FULFILLMENT"), and he is ranked together with such giants as Phidias, Michelangelo, and Aeschylus, "complete fulfillment" is unattainable even by the greatest artist. "The stigma of this globe is—want: / FULFILLMENT? . . . hurts it!" Near-perfection is almost static; it is frozen into harmony. Without a built-in element of imperfection the development of human culture and art would be impossible, and this is the very principle on which the dialectic of history rests. It is reasonable to suppose that Norwid was preoccupied with the problem which could be characterized as "the necessity of imperfection" in the same way as some theologians were considering the "necessity of evil," and that his attitude to this paradox was somewhat ambivalent. At any rate, in his eyes Chopin came as near to perfection as any Polish artist could in the nineteenth century.

Chopin's supreme creative achievement was now about to be defiled and symbolically ruined by barbarians. Stanza VIII telescopes our attention on Warsaw where this event takes place. In 1863 during the Polish Insurrection, an attempt was made on the life of Count Berg, Governor-General of Poland. As a reprisal the Warsaw palace of the Zamoyskis was ransacked and set on fire by the Cossacks. Chopin's piano, kept in the palace, was flung out the window by them. Stanza IX is a visionary description of this scene ending with "a coffin-like" object falling from the window which the poet recognizes as Chopin's piano.

The last stanza repeats the fact that this piano which evoked Poland "at the zenith of complete perfection in history" was destroyed, thrown to the pavement. The Orpheus motif, which occurred in the second stanza, returns here with full force:

> And behold: how man's noble thought
> Is trampled upon by human fury,
> Just as—*since the beginning of*
> *Time—everything that awakens the soul!*
> And—behold—it is like Orpheus's body
> Torn to pieces by a thousand Passions . . .

The destruction of Chopin's piano is the symbolic martyrdom of art aspiring to higher things and of human creativity as well. Yet this martyrdom (which is, as the quoted passage shows, strangely ritualized), for all its tragic overtones, gives hope. In the last four lines of the poem there is certainly more than a simple expression of despair or bitterness over the suppression of the

1863 uprising and the fate of Chopin's piano. These lines end the poem in a somewhat enigmatic, that is, very Norwid-like, manner:

> But you? but I?—let us strike up a song of atonement
> Exhorting: *"Distant grandson, rejoice!* . . ."
> *The dumb stones—groaned aloud:*
> *The ideal has reached the pavement"*—24

The interpretation of this text has usually centered on the last line—in Polish: *"Ideał—sięgnął bruku—"*. Some critics stressing the fact that the Ideal *crashed* to the ground see it as Norwid's disappointment on account of the failure of the 1863 uprising, while others believe that the poet was hoping for the elevation of the poor (symbolized by the pavement) to the Ideal, and that the enigmatic "distant grandson, rejoice!" refers to the age when not only the chosen few but all people will understand Chopin's music and Norwid's ideals. Both these interpretations are somewhat forced and one falls back on a third, more balanced one, according to which in the encounter of Ideal and Matter (the pavement) Norwid saw the inevitable law of historical development, "the victory of the truth of Diogenes." 25 This view could be further expanded. As a rule *sądne pienie* is translated as "Doomsday song" or "the Doomsday dirge"; but is this event so truly apocalyptic that it should warrant such an expression? It is more likely that Norwid used this adjective in another sense, having in mind the Jewish Day of Atonement. But for what should Norwid and the poet-addressee Antoni Czajkowski of *Chopin's Piano* atone? For the sins, for the individual and historical mistakes of mankind, for killing Orpheus (and Christ), for the ritual act of murdering God committed symbolically through the destruction of the Ideal. Clearly, the advice to future generations to rejoice stands in direct relationship to the fact that this new "orphic" sacrifice had already taken place, that the Ideal did hit the ground. This historical optimism grows out of Norwid's belief in mankind's future course, its gradual perfection; its decline now is so complete that a spiritual regeneration cannot be too far away. One has to rejoice for two reasons: because in the fall of the Ideal the law was fulfilled and because as in another poem of Norwid's where "the cross became a gate," this sacrificial rite opened up the way to the future.

The Lyric Poet

In its formal aspects *Chopin's Piano* is much more experimental than the rest of *Vade-Mecum*. It is written in a rhyming free verse, with frequent changes of rhythm; the lines vary in length and are sometimes broken up into very short emotive phrases. Apart from the historial and cultural associations discussed earlier, the poem also contains an impressionistic reflection of Chopin's music; certain elements of Chopin's style such as "the whispering tone" and the "impromptu" chords are woven into the texture of Norwid's poem as well. In fact, the entire poem seems to have been composed on musical principles; when read aloud it sounds like a piece of music written for the instrument of the *vox humana*. Nevertheless, the euphonic elements do not outweigh the content; they do not merely embellish but bring out and amplify "the message." In its subject matter as well as in its execution this is an original and striking poem. It remains among the best lyric achievements of Norwid and of the whole post-Romantic period.

V   *Poetry is Dead*

Vade-Mecum was not published in Norwid's lifetime. Brockhaus, the Leipzig publisher who had already brought out a volume of Norwid's poems earlier, did offer a contract for a second volume, but in 1866 backed out of his commitment for financial and political reasons. This was a heavy blow, for it was not the first time that Norwid had suffered from the adverse consequences of a sudden political change. The first phase of his poetic career, which reached its peak with *Promethidion* and such outstanding poems as the one written to General Bem, was overshadowed by the suppression of the 1848 revolutions and the consolidation of reactionary forces all over Europe. The uprising in Poland in 1863–64 was one of the reasons which prevented the wider distribution of his work, thus forestalling even a moderate success for Norwid's first collection of poetry. In 1866 preparations for the Prusso-Austrian war made Brockhaus rescind his earlier offer to Norwid.

The period that followed was one of almost continuous gloom in Norwid's life, only occasionally brightened by such episodes as the warm reception of *A Poem about the Freedom of the Word* (*Rzecz o wolności słowa*) read by the poet himself to a Polish émigré audience in Paris, or his romantic friendship with the attractive and intelligent Zofia Węgierska. With Węgierska's sudden death Norwid became more lonely and misanthropic than ever before; his living conditions worsened to the point of periodic starvation, destitution inevitably causing ill health and long periods of depression. By 1870 Norwid must have been almost totally deaf, as at the time of the Franco-Prussian war he was dismissed from the French National Guard for not being able to understand the orders of the commanding officer. Two years later the first signs of tuberculosis appeared; he was coughing blood. Poor living conditions and undernourishment weakened his constitution year by year and, finally, the lack of interest in his literary work and the scarcity of commissions for drawings and paintings forced him into the dreaded situation which he had been determined to avoid at all costs. After an unsuccessful attempt to escape from Paris to Florence which failed owing to the lack of adequate financial support expected from a Polish aristocrat, in 1877 Norwid had to accept the offer of a distant relative and move to the St. Casimir Asylum, a home for destitute and elderly Polish émigrés on the outskirts of Paris. Here a broken and tired Norwid lived the last six years of his life in constantly failing health and growing bitterness.

The poetic output of these last years was much smaller than that of the period preceding *Vade-Mecum*, especially in the field of lyric poetry, for Norwid wrote several epic poems after 1865 (*A Poem about the Freedom of the Word, Assunta, A Dorio ad Phrygium*) and these included his most successful works in this particular genre. Apparently after the completion of *Vade-Mecum* Norwid's interest had turned toward other literary forms: he wrote plays and essays and proved his ability as a writer of narrative prose as well. Lyric poems were written on the side, almost marginally if at all; Norwid kept himself busy with other—literary and linguistic, scholarly and artistic—activities.

The tone of the old Norwid's lyric is a shade darker even than that of the gloomier pieces of *Vade-Mecum*. If he had been an ironic observer and caustic critic of Western and Polish society earlier, now he became a tragic outcast from that society of "money and blood" which never gave him a chance to prove himself. The occasional visitor saw in him a failure: a quaint mixture of an embittered misanthropist and an unsuccessful artist. He himself often doubted the sense of his lonely and increasingly frustrated efforts to break through the indifference of his contemporaries. In 1876 he wrote to a fellow-émigré: "Emigration stripped me of everything: my youth, my strength, *my personal friends,* it took away the value, almost the very names of my ancestors and the honor of their names. If this had happened for some reason—I would not be surprised and I would respect it— but for *nothing!*—because they haven't done ANYTHING. . . ." [26] Norwid's correspondence from these years is full of bitter and scathing words about his compatriots, but the French and other Europeans do not fare much better either. Indeed, in the short run, Norwid had no cause for optimism, either personally or historically; the failure of the 1863 uprising proved him right when he opposed armed action in unfavorable conditions and foretold that Poland's liberation would take place only in the distant future. The events of 1870–71 showed that his deep mistrust of one-sided progress, the Progress-God of the Positivists, was perfectly justified; without real social and political progress the industrial-technological boom only exacerbated the class struggle. Railways helped human communications, but the various strata of society had very little to communicate to each other. In his last years Norwid's protests against the cult of money and against the gross insensitivity of the rich bourgeois grew in fury and intensity. In this respect the Third Republic was no better than the Second Empire; in fact, it demolished even the last vestiges of the old hierarchy. Norwid's attitude is clear from his stories written after 1871, but it is discernible from the general tone of his poems as well. One of these points to the conflicts that ultimately led to the First World War, a possibility more or less foreseen by the ailing old émigré in Paris:

> And there will be great Progress! it will rejuvenate
> The world, evening out the map of Europe like velvet,
> Strategically and smoothly, as a result of the "Eastern question"—
> There'll be nations in arms—and the famous General Dynamite! [27]

While Norwid's skepticism as to a better future based on the progress of industry, railways, and the stock-exchange was growing, he was also becoming more selective in the choice of his heroes. In a world which admired bankers and Bismarcks, extolled the use of armed might, and encouraged the rise of revolutionary terror, he was looking in vain for people of the stature and qualities of a General Bem, a John Brown, or even an Adam Mickiewicz. The freedom-loving heroes of his youth were not expelled from the Pantheon of his memory, but he came to see Garibaldi's march on Rome as a tragic error and the communards of 1871 as mindless barbarians. In fact, of all the political personalities of this decade, there remained only one to whom he could still address a poem: Pope Pius IX. Norwid was always careful in defining his approval of a popular hero; for example, in 1860 while hailing Mickiewicz and Kossuth as great popular leaders, he added the qualification: "but of these people [Mickiewicz, Kossuth and O'Connell] perhaps O'Connell alone has my real sympathy." [28] His preference for political moderates and reformers did not change in later years; if anything, it became more marked. In the year of the Franco-Prussian war he wrote to Zaleski: "And if O'Connell and the Pope had not done a few things, the year 1848 would have been not what it was but an *abominatio-desolationis!* . . . If the Pope and O'Connell *had not given a moral content to the aspirations toward progress and freedom* then 1848, in spite of its barricades (a childish thing) would not have left behind the abolition of the death sentence for political offences. . . ." [29]

The passage quoted shows how defensive Norwid had become in political arguments with friends, how difficult he found it to accept radical Leftism as an alternative to the status quo which he strongly disliked. On the other hand, neither the national nor the "liberal Catholic" hopes of the author of *Promethidion* came closer to realization between 1849 and 1870. As for the Paris Commune, its excesses shocked and frightened Norwid and made him raise a public protest on various issues, thus risking imprisonment. But even if "God and parliamentarianism" managed to save the French people from anarchy, the Third Republic was only the lesser of two evils, not an achievement of any kind. As for Poland, Russian repressions continued for many years after 1864 and included a policy of deliberate Russification. The only part of Poland which seemed to present a slightly brighter picture was Austrian-ruled Cracow and Galicia, and it is no accident that, when after 1870 Norwid considered the possibility of returning to Poland, he thought of settling in Galicia.

Loneliness, bad health, and a feeling of revulsion at the unscrupulous commercialism and opportunism of society form the background to one of the more important poems written by Norwid in the last decade of his life: *On the Death of Poetry (Na zgon poezji).* Poetry has died, having fallen victim to a wasting disease called "money and scribbles." She is mourned by the poet as if she were a living person whose loss has left a feeling of sadness, never felt before. (It has been suggested that the first version of this poem was written soon after the death of Zofia Węgierska—hence the unusual personification of "Poetry.") On a more symbolic plane, the death of poetry can mean either that industrial society interested only in money-making and cheap novels kills any higher form of art or that poetry has died in the soul of the poet with his "life imprisonment" behind the walls of the St. Casimir Asylum. The latter explanation would clarify a line toward the end of the poem in which Norwid blames the "destroyers of thought"—those responsible for the annihilation of the spirit of poetry.

This, however, was not the poet's last word. Two years later in a poetic letter addressed to Bronisław Zaleski (*Do Bronisława Z.*), where among other things he recalled his conversations on matters of art with Michelet and Mickiewicz, Norwid once again reiterated the credo of his life in a simple, dignified, almost axiomatic manner:

Abundance of all kinds will disappear, fade away,
Treasures and power will be swept away, whole people will tremble,
Of the things of this world only two will remain,
Two only: *poetry and goodness* . . . nothing else . . .[30]

This is the essence of Norwid's poetic message. He was a staunch believer to the very end, believing not only in the resurrection of the body and the survival of the spirit taught by the Church but also in the resurrection of *his word* in the future—a rediscovery of his work by unborn generations. Few people possess such a strong faith; but in his case it was justified. Norwid, this "specialist in the code of existence," was rediscovered at the end of the nineteenth century and published by Zenon Przesmycki, and his reputation has steadily grown throughout our century. At present, one hundred and fifty years after his birth, he is the only nineteenth-century poet still regarded by Polish poets as their contemporary. It is not simply his biography and personal legend that impresses them, but his overall achievement as a writer and poet. His ideas and allegiances are still debated; he is often drawn upon as a source of moral and linguistic sensibility. Mickiewicz and Słowacki are classics, Norwid is modern. He is admired, imitated, denounced, and dissected; Norwid the lyric poet is still very much alive.

CHAPTER 4

Narrative and Longer Poems

I Quidam

THE narrative poem enjoyed considerable popularity among
Romantics. Byron with his colorful and exciting tales influenced a whole generation of Polish poets: both Mickiewicz's
Konrad Wallenrod and Słowacki's *Beniowski* would have been
unimaginable without Byron's example. Norwid, whose poetry
grew out of the Romantic tradition evolving toward a unique
kind of post-Romantic Symbolism, also felt the challenge of this
genre. The two models which impressed him most were probably Byron's *Childe Harold* and Słowacki's *Journey to the Holy
Land*. Both these narrative poems were poetic tales, and Norwid's
first attempt in the genre, the slight *Wedding (Wesele)* written in
1847, was subtitled "a tale" as well. His later work included
kinds of longer poems other than the straightforward narrative.
Apart from "tales" he also wrote long philosophical poems or
verse treatises like *Promethidion, Slavery (Niewola)* and *A Poem
about the Freedom of the Word (Rzecz o wolności słowa)*; narrative poems interspersed with lyric fragments (*Assunta, A Dorio ad
Phrygium*); and, finally, epic parables (*przypowieści*) such as
Epimenides and *Quidam*. This classification cannot be applied to
all Norwid's longer poems. Sometimes the poet himself added to
"generic" confusion by subtitling two very different kinds of
poems as "rhapsody," but it covers his most important work in
this genre.

The first ambitious long poem after the hostile critical reception of *Promethidion* was undoubtedly *Quidam*. The idea of an
epic poem about the world of antiquity had been maturing in
Norwid's mind for many years, ever since his studies in Italy and
extensive excursions around the Mediterranean. *Pompeii (Pom-
peja, 1848 or 1849)*, an unfinished poem set against the background of the Roman ghost town, was the first to express Nor-

wid's special interest in Greco-Roman culture, in the life and problems of imperial Rome, which created a civilization impressive in its material wealth and artistic achievements but doomed by its failure to defeat or effectively absorb its two main adversaries: the Christians and the barbarians. Norwid's admiration for Greco-Roman culture was a natural extension of his Christian historiosophy. After all, Greek philosophy, Roman law, and historiography provided the intellectual background to the beginnings of the Christian religion. We know from his writings how powerfully this early Christianity, a faith not yet debased by worldly interests, appealed to Norwid's imagination. Moreover, the first century after Christ was an age of great chiliastic expectations and powerful uprisings against Rome, easily lending itself as a parallel with the nineteenth century with its vast social upheavals and widespread expectations among radicals of the Universal War against tyranny. Norwid recognized this, but only during his American interlude, where with a more detached perspective of the past and the present of European civilization, did he begin to write *Quidam,* his parable on a Roman theme.

Though the theme was Roman, the message was partly Polish. *Quidam* represents Norwid's last literary reflections on the fate of his "orphaned generation," a chain of reflections started in Rome and continued in Paris between 1849 and 1852. *Quidam* was designed to be a symbolic farewell to the Romantic age and the vision of a new one, requiring a novel, different type of heroism:

> *So it was meant to be the picture of a generation*
> *Which, on the eve of the revelation of Christian truth,*
> *Between the sunset of Greek and Jewish wisdom*
> *Grows wildly and perishes like a herb at a balk. . . .*[1]

The scene is Rome in the years A.D. 132 and 133. Emperor Hadrian reigns over the multilingual empire. Norwid takes great care in re-creating the atmosphere of the Rome of this period. Not only is everyday life painted in sometimes painstaking detail, but the characters of the protagonists also exhibit realistic traits. They are much less Romantic and exalted than, for instance, the heroes of Krasiński's *Irydion,* also a "Roman" tragedy, which constituted a challenge and a constant point of reference for Norwid. In fact, Norwid was aware of the "unglamorous"

nature of his main heroes. He pointed out in the introduction to
Quidam that he called the poem a "parable" since he consciously
avoided "the plot, characteristic of the poetic tale." [2]

The central hero, then, is not an outstanding personality, but
simply *quidam:* "someone," someone and perhaps everyone. In
Norwid's poem there are two Quidams: a young poet from Epi-
reus who comes to Rome, falls in love with Sophie the beautiful
half-Greek maiden, and is killed through a misunderstanding. His
involvement in a scuffle is interpreted as sacrilege by the crowd
and by the pagan priest chasing a sacrificial animal through a
public square, and he is killed, his death being purely accidental.
The other Quidam, also known as the gardener Guido, is a Christian. He embodies the new type of heroism by defying the Emperor's despotic power and by standing up against the mob after
the unwarranted murder of the other Quidam. He is identified
as a Christian, is seized, and will probably die a martyr's death,
but *his* death will not be meaningless: it sows the seeds of a new
world.

The plot in *Quidam* is barely sketched and the whole poem,
written in regularly rhyming verse of the eleven-syllable line, is
full of enigmatic references and allusions. Three main threads
running through the poem nevertheless can be distinguished:
there is a love thread (Quidam-Epirote — Sophie), a political
thread (Hadrian — Magus Jason — Arthemidor), and a religious
thread (Rome versus the Jews and the Christians). As in *Irydion,*
a deep difference exists between those who want to destroy
Rome's power by violent means and those who eventually will
succeed in destroying and transforming Rome through their individual martyrdom and anonymous sacrifice. This conflict has been
interpreted in a way which relates it to Norwid's biography. According to this view the Rome of Hadrian can be seen as the
Rome of 1847–1848 and the chief protagonists of *Quidam* as Norwid's contemporaries.[3] Thus Sophie, the beautiful but cold half-
Greek poetess, resembling the formal perfection of an empty
Greek vase, would be in part modeled after Maria Kalergis.
Arthemidor, the Greek philosopher who had "his own school"
and taught dialectics but was blind to "the essence of the Uni-
verse," corresponds roughly to Zygmut Krasiński, whom after
their quarrel in 1849 Norwid still admired but also scorned for
his "Platonism." A darkly compelling character is Jason, the Jew-

ish Magus, who coaches his disciples for the next uprising in Judea and who believes that one of these young men will become the new Messiah—he is a mixture of Towiański and Mickiewicz. (The Towianists often referred to their master in prophetic terms, calling him a new Moses destined "to deliver the Polish nation from slavery" and we know from Norwid's correspondence that he regarded the Towiański group as a "Cabbalistic sect.") [4] On the other hand, the Magus and Arthemidor share certain traits: "The common people saw a secret in these two men / Which linked them into one giant. . . ." [5] This description indicates that, perhaps, Mickiewicz was the chief model for Magus Jason.

As for Norwid himself, he could be both Quidams simultaneously. Thus the young Epirote with his unrequited love for Sophie is a poet, who might stand for Norwid's poetic self and, though the character behaves intuitively in a Christian manner, is "not yet reborn" in Christ's spirit. While Guido, the gardener, could be regarded as the ideal toward which Norwid is striving, part of the mature Norwid ("the artist-worker") is already "Guido," that is, fully Christian. His Christian faith makes Guido "supranational" by definition; this is also in accord with Norwid's conviction that one has to be "first a man and only then a Pole"— Christianity takes precedence over nationalism.

During his voluntary exile within the exile, his stay in the United States, Norwid once again turned to the Bible, which became for him a great source of consolation in hours of extreme loneliness.[6] His thorough reading of the Bible, especially of the New Testament, affected the author of *Quidam* in more than one way. He began now to formulate a new concept of heroism which one could describe as "apostolic," and he began to apply the *parable* as a method of artistic creation much more frequently than before. Quidam-Epirote "does not act, he only seeks and desires goodness and truth," [7] but his alter ego, Guido, is ready to act, is ready to denounce the sinfulness of innocently spilt blood. This is the conscious act of a Christian defying pagan law and standing up against a hostile majority. Quidam-Guido's declaration of faith Norwid values higher than the sacrifice of nationalistic revolutionaries (the disciples of Magus Jason) conceived in a spirit of hatred and revenge. All the characters of *Quidam* are "ruins of the past"; only Guido represents something that belongs to the future. This is one of the more obvious meanings of Norwid's "parable."

For it is not, in spite of realistic descriptions of houses, landscapes or garments, an easily comprehensible narrative poem. The action is often interrupted by interpolations such as a "scroll" of a poem written by Quidam-Epirote or an improvisation by Sophie. At other times the author indulges in philosophical digressions, which seem superfluous from a preconceived "structural" point of view, or he makes allusions which are only in part explained by his own footnotes. While the historical background and the social microrealism of *Quidam* are convincing (Norwid seems to know everything about the way people had lived and communicated in Hadrian's Rome, and he attaches special importance to people's gestures), the work as a whole suffers from its lack of a coherent plot and its unexplained tragic endings. All the main characters disappear or die for different reasons, or for no valid reason at all. The Epirote dies accidentally; Guido is to die as a Christian martyr; but why is Sophie poisoned and by whom? Bar-Kochba, Jason's disciple, dies in the battle, but why should Jason die at the moment when he receives the Emperor's letter banishing him from Rome? What was Norwid's aim with this undramatic sequence of tragic deaths? *Quidam* is full of white spots and vague allusions. In spite of the perspicacity of some observations and the undisputed beauty of a few lyric fragments, this "parable" of Norwid has remained one of his least popular works.

II Felice: *A Byronesque Tale*

After *Quidam*, and another, shorter and less important, narrative poem, *Epimenides*, Norwid tried his pen at the poetic tale and wrote *Szczesna* which, thanks to the successful mediation of a friend, was printed in 1859 at St. Petersburg soon after its completion. *Szczesna* (an approximate English translation of this feminine name would be "Felice") is the closest to a Byronic poem ever written by Norwid, though it is Byron as imitated by Słowacki in his *Journey to the Holy Land*. Like Słowacki's poem, *Felice* is written in sestinas, plus twenty-four lines of the same length, and part of it describes the hero's travels. The core of the plot is, however, the unhappy love affair of Szczesny (Felix) with his namesake Szczesna. The tale, consisting of an introduction or inovation in verse and of four parts, is constructed in a peculiar manner. The first part or "background" is one long digression, full of irony at the expense of the "sensitive reader" who expects romances but shuns "the blood and sweat" of real life. He is also expected to dislike anything that is hard to understand, so the poet assures him that he will write in the "most reasonable" manner. This is followed in Song II by a description of Felice, which—though not lacking in relevant information such as: "she was beautiful, rich, clever, powerful and young"—still leaves the reader dissatisfied, for the author consciously avoids a physical description. The next song is an impressionistic account of an encounter at Felice's house, ending with Felix's departure for abroad. Only in the last song does the action gather speed as Felix follows Norwid's itinerary from Berlin through Paris and Italy to the other side of the Atlantic. Each stanza is a letter, or a fragment of a letter, written from a different town or locality, the ninth and last being Felix's ironical congratulation to his unfaithful fiancée upon learning of her impending marriage to another man:

> My lady! . . . so you are to be married and your first
> Thought is of me? . . . I solemnly send you my best
> Wishes!—my heart, my soul and nerves
> Welcome the flower sent in your letter . . .
> Today I cannot write more—someone is waiting—
> Just two words: I remember . . . I love . . . WHAT IS HUMAN.[8]

In other words Norwid's disillusioned lover does not want to remember either his ex-fiancée's social status or her weakness and inconstancy. Only what is best in her, her essence as a human being, will be preserved in the hero's memory. This impassioned, though also ironical, confession somewhat changes Szczesny's image, for until now he has seemed to be a typical Romantic traveler, studying philosophy in Berlin, praying in Rome, and describing the terrible poverty of the simple folk in Calabria. Szczesna-Felice has remained in the backgkround, as a link with the hero's native country, a person respected and remembered rather than passionately loved. This detachment which is bridged only in the last—farewell—letter might be a stylization, but it might also be an accurate description of the relationship on which Szczesna is based. This is Norwid's youthful love and engagement to Kamilla L. B. who in the poet's own words "truly loved me—for a short time." J. W. Gomulicki corroborates this hypothesis with some interesting evidence, among which the striking correspondence of Christian names (Kamil—the poet's second name received at his confirmation—Kamilla; Szczesny-Szczesna) is stressed together with the similarity between Felix's and Norwid's own situation soon after leaving Poland.[9] In other words, the last song of the poem can be read as autobiographical with one reservation: Norwid certainly had no *groom* or servant to accompany him on his journeys.

Szczesna was conventional enough to be liked better by Polish readers than other, more intellectually demanding, works of Norwid. It was reprinted in the poet's lifetime and paraphrased into German by a translator well before Norwid's rediscovery. Although it contains gems of wit and some good metaphors, it does not stand comparison with Słowacki's *Journey to the Holy Land*, not even with *Assunta*, another poetic tale written by Norwid some years later. *Szczesna* is inferior to *Assunta* both in construction and poetic values. There was, perhaps too much of a conscious effort involved in writing *Szczesna*, a wish to entertain on the part of a poet whose nature had consistently gravitated toward serious themes and moral problems.

III *The Progress of the Word*

Without a discussion, however brief, of Norwid's views on language and the nature of his linguistic interest, it is almost impossible to give a critical interpretation of one of his most ambitious epic poems, entitled *A Poem about the Freedom of the Word* (*Rzecz o wolności słowa*).

Norwid's special interest in language was not unusual. Already the first generation of Romantics had "discovered" language as the root of all philosophy and poetry and placed it into the center of its critical enquiries. Following Vico, Herder, and the Schlegel brothers, the analytical study of language became popular in the Congress Kingdom and in other parts of partitioned Poland as well, though "linguistics" often meant obsessive etymologizing rather than the discipline of descriptive grammar. Among the Polish writers and scholars who in the first half of the nineteenth century made a special effort to unravel the mysteries of language, Jan Nepomucen Kamiński (1777–1855) occupied a special place. Kamiński, author of popular plays and poems as well as the Director of the Polish Theatre in Lwów (Lvov), was at the same time an enthusiastic amateur linguist. His linguistic studies, including a piece entitled "Is Our Language Philosophical?" (*Czy język nasz jest filozoficzny?*), published in contemporary reviews won him many admirers, among them such talented people as the outstanding Romantic critic Maurycy Mochnacki. Mochnacki, and after him Norwid, described Kamiński as a "genius"—a view not shared by later, more positivistic-minded scholars who characterized Kamiński's main linguistic work *The Soul Considered as Thought, Word, and Sign* (*Dusza uważana jako myśl, słowo i znak*, Lwów, 1851) as "consisting of psychological and etymological games . . . which have nothing in common either with truth or with scientific theories." [10] Yet there is good reason to believe that Norwid, who read his Mochnacki carefully and, in general, agreed with most of his critical judgments, was also influenced by Kamiński's theories and linguistic practice. Norwid's frequent attempts to find and/or restore the original meaning of a word (its "primary-form") and his notorious predilection for neologisms of a "philosophical" type certainly indicate such an influence. Although Norwid's special interest in language became manifest only in the 1850's, after *Promethidion* some of his critics already considered Norwid and the sage of Lwów birds of the same feather; both were equally hard to understand. [11]

Nevertheless, when Norwid became engaged in the pursuit of solving linguistic riddles, he was also following a very old tradition. The philosophical justification of his cult of the Word, as for many Romantics before him, was derived from the first verse of The Gospel of John: "In the beginning was the Word and the Word was with God and the Word was God." The word and its form of expression—human speech—were of divine origin. This concept formed, among other ideas, a basic part of Ballanche's teaching as well. The word was given to mankind as a gift to further its progress, and it is only through work and the creative use of the word that such progress is possible. The special significance of the word had been first expounded by Norwid in *The Word and the Letter* (*Słowo i litera*), an unfinished treatise written 'as early as 1851. From this text it transpires that man's duality, the inevitable disharmony between form and content experienced by him, can be bridged only by the human word.

Already here, Norwid shows his interest in the history of the word. With the invention of the alphabet, he maintains, the Phoenicians brought about "the first revolution" of the word. Until this event only "the word of the race" had existed, but henceforth, and especially with the appearance of Christianity, a new entity was born—"the word of the nation" (*słowo-narodu*) which "embodied the many-sidedness of its [the nation's] thought." [12] There exists one even higher level: the "word of a civilization" which expresses a whole epoch. Sometimes these are expressed by more than one nation; for instance, although Greek civilization was a great accomplishment in itself, Greek thought was fully expressed only in Roman law. Unfortunately, the text abruptly ends with the discussion and criticism of Roman architecture.

As can be seen from the summary of this treatise, Norwid operates with an esoteric and ambiguous terminology. His "word" means many things and is used in a highly figurative fashion. Furthermore there is a complex relationship between "the spirit," "the word," and "the letter." The letter of the alphabet is a link between the inner and the physical world, between the Spirit and reality, the word being "the spirit of the letter." The deeper the Spirit penetrates the letter and the more organic their relationship becomes, the more perfect is the work of art resulting from this union. This explains why in *A Poem about the Freedom of the Word* Norwid puts such emphasis on the correct perception and understanding of "the letter."

A Poem about the Freedom of the Word was written in 1869 and first recited by the poet himself in May of the same year at a meeting of the Polish Committee of the Society of Aid for Scholars. That evening, at which most émigré literati and intellectuals were present, became one of the rare public triumphs in Norwid's life. The audience gave a warm reception to the recital of his long poetic treatise, and, eventually, funds were raised to publish it. Unfortunately for the poet, the success remained artistic and moral; it never brought him any money. Working on the poem involved "the neglect of all other interests," and events connected with the publication of the manuscript—the printer's losing several pages, which Norwid had to rewrite in a hurry—further increased the author's frustration. Still worse, history once again "overtook" Norwid, as within a few months of the publication of *A Poem about the Freedom of the Word* the Franco-Prussian war broke out and eliminated all possible financial expectations the unfortunate poet may have had in connection with his booklet.

The concept behind Norwid's long poem is ambitious, although perhaps not as much as Victor Hugo's intention in writing *La Légende des Siècles*, in which he wanted "to express mankind in a cyclical work . . . in all its aspects [such as] history, fable, philosophy, religion and science."[13] We know that Norwid admired Hugo's talent and considered the French poet one of the poetic giants of the century, but the only similarity between the two epic poems is a historiosophic not a stylistic one. While *La Légende des Siècles* is a cycle of smaller epic pieces, each dramatically constructed around a person or a situation, *A Poem about the Freedom of the Word* is frankly didactic, somewhat reminiscent of versed treatises popular in the eighteenth century. It is written in a traditional form of rhymed couplets with thirteen-syllable lines and consists of fourteen parts of varying length, the only unifying factor being the time sequence, as Norwid follows the development of the Word throughout history. Since his method is not simply descriptive but involves numerous digressions of a theoretical and historiosophic nature, *A Poem about the Freedom of the Word* can be called one of the most important single sources for Norwid's views on the dialectic of history. Parts X to XIII reflect the poet's thoughts on the then contemporary situation. Here, once again, Norwid appears less a learned student of the past and more a social and cultural critic of society.

In his introduction to the poem Norwid makes it clear that he is not concerned with freedom of speech, but with the freedom of the Word. Part I demonstrates Norwid's belief in the divine aim and mission of the word. Just as "mankind without divinity betrays itself," just as a naked and lonely human being can be insignificant and miserable, so the word can be misunderstood and ignored in itself. However, it becomes powerful when it acts as an agent of human history. And its function and significance, says Norwid, is different in the case of each nation. This is a historicist's view, although in Part II the poet takes issue with Darwin and the evolutionists: "The wise men of today declare— and have their docile listeners— / That *Man* is but the next link in the chain / Of creation . . ."[14] and that his evolution took place in a spontaneous manner due to natural selection. Norwid declares his opposition by giving more credit to the "naive legends of Mankind" and accepting the traditional view of man's creation. He was created "complete" and lost this completeness through the Fall. As for religion, man has a deep innate need for it born of "man . . . seeking the roots of his own loneliness." Human speech began with the monologue and evolved through the dialogue to the "choral" or collective speech. Since the fateful episode of Babel, however, he sees two different traditions existing side by side and hinging upon the use of the "inner word": these are the traditions of Moses and of Prometheus. Moses preached to the family and the clan, Prometheus to "distant relatives"—to all members of the human brotherhood. The "inner word" has often lost its weight and sanctity, has often deteriorated, waning into mere formulas. Whenever this has happened a monster has appeared on the scene—"the hyena of slavery." This is what befell the Jewish nation after the Golden Age of David (whose *Psalms* Norwid regarded as a masterpiece of world literature), and this is what happened to most nations in the epoch before Christ's birth when the whole world shared one great desire—that the Word should come to life. Christ came and became the starting point of the new age; through Him not divinity but "humanity was revealed to the people." Yet the highest point in the development of the word came after Christ, with Saint Paul. He is a hero very close to Norwid's heart, but here we are concerned only with his objective role. According to Norwid in Paul's writings "the Word returned into the spirit and became complete." [15] Since then nothing really new has happened, except for different tribes and languages accepting the heritage of Christianity. Parts I to IX are a survey of the past evolution of the word from the beginnings of mankind to the birth of the institutionalized Christian religion.

As to the tone of Norwid's criticism of present conditions expressed in Parts X to XIII of the treatise, this does not differ greatly from the all-pervasive irony of *Vade-Mecum*. In the contemporary world the word has been debased; anything that is topical is good and "books are racing like bicycles" to reach an ever growing audience. The age is full of "vulgarizers"; it is their attitude to the word that differentiates and separates them from "real authors." Many of the "vulgarizers" are extremely easy to understand, but this does not prove their superiority. On the contrary: "The author *enters darkness* to wrest the light, / The vulgarizer enters *light* in order to shed it for a background. . . ." [16] The latter is not interested in new truth, which can be conquered only if one penetrates "the darkness" of life. Unlike Norwid, the vulgarizer regards the word as a tool, not as an aim in itself; he does not believe in the sanctity of the word.

In Part XII, after these linguistic-philosophical considerations, the problem of "the letter" comes up. The Polish language, asserts Norwid, is deficient on this issue, since it fails to realise the importance of the printed letter, the fact that "the letter is *an equivalent part of the word.*" This "unfaithfulness" to the letter results in an inability "to give." Other cultures, though less rich or original than the Polish, give more to the world. Polish culture is a series of great eruptions of creative energy without any historical continuity. Norwid contrasts here the powerful and magnificent eruption of a volcano (so characteristic of the Romantic method of creation) with the long, patient, slow work of a great river which is not less majestic and is certainly more useful in its immediate results. This is the work-style of the classicist and also of the post-Romantic artist; this is also Norwid's program.

The past of the Polish language forms the subject matter of Part XIII. In its first few stanzas Norwid evokes the immense work, the humble effort of generations of people which between the fourteenth and sixteenth centuries spread the Polish language all over the territory of the *Respublica*. This effort produced the miracle of Czarnolas, the rich and supple poetic idiom of the poet Kochanowski. In the following stanzas Norwid makes a digression and attempts a poetic etymology of the word "Slav"—he connects the Polish word for a "Slav" (*Słowianin*) with *Sclavus*, *sława* and *słowo*. He does not accept the earlier false etymology which took *słowo* (word) for the root of *Słowianin* but plays on the similarity of the words *Sclavi* (Slavs) and *słaby* (weak). When the Word became a real power in the world with Christ and the spread of the Gospel, the former slaves and the weak ones felt their strength for the first time. The implicit message of this play on words is the same as of the earlier parts: Christ and his gospel were the greatest revelation in human history.

The Slavs perceived the Word and embraced the faith but did not pay attention to the letter. This negligence had serious con-

sequences; not only the lack of continuity referred to earlier, but
such defects of the Polish language as "a dubious orthography, a
muddled punctuation / To this day a foreign or a poor nomencla-
ture . . . / The forms of discussion so scantily worked out / That
it is hard to disagree, much easier to step aside. . . ." [17] Poland,
Norwid continues, is a country where whatever happens is
doomed to be soon forgotten. It is a country where "yes—everything exists . . . somewhere . . . somehow . . . and gets lost." This
is a strikingly modern critique of Polish conditions. Norwid, when
he implies a certain "vagueness of forms," has in mind the unde-
veloped forms of social conflict and social activity. The same
theme was taken up and developed by Witold Gombrowicz, a
twentieth-century writer, when explaining the reasons for his
rebellion against "Polishness," [18] although probably he did not
read *A Poem about the Freedom of the Word*.

The last part of this long epic poem is a vision of the ruins of
Palmyra, a symbol which may be interpreted in more than one
way. The ruins are "an entity" complete in themselves. They
should not be destroyed, for their completeness is beautiful.
Should one build on the ruins, or rebuild these ruins? What do
the ruins of Palmyra stand for? All these are open questions. According to one possibility, Norwid is against social evolutionism
of the Darwinian kind. He is only for progress that would accept
the "completeness of the past" as a starting point. Another possibility is that all the words of the past are in fact ruins and one
should go on building (writing), though the result will be, no
doubt, another ruin which will seem complete only from the
vantage point of the future.

A Poem about the Freedom of the Word is one of Norwid's
more difficult works. Without an interest in history, philosophy,
and linguistics the contemporary reader might find this long poem
tiring and tedious. If, however, we regard it as a rhymed essay
rather than a poetic entertainment of the *Don Juan* type, it is not
difficult to find merit in its rich texture of thought and idiosyncratic language. The latter is in constant struggle with linguistic
convention, for Norwid makes a great effort to express his thought
both succinctly and precisely. In parts of the poem he succeeds
well, and even where he only approaches but fails to reach this
ideal, his is an honorable failure.

IV Assunta

"It has been correctly observed that in Polish literature there are but few long love poems (*poematy miłosne*). . . . The only ones are *The Forefathers' Eve Part I* and Słowacki's *In Switzerland*—two for a whole literature! As for Malczewski's *Maria*, it is a tale." [19] These sentences from the author's short introduction to his *Assunta, or The Glance* (*Assunta: czyli Spojrzenie*) show Norwid's desire to fill a gap in Polish literature. What they also show is Norwid's awareness of the poetic stature he could claim by virtue of *Vade-Mecum* and the rest of his *oeuvre*. He wrote the first version of *Assunta* in 1870 (revising and retouching it again in 1877 and 1879) at a time when his creative powers stood, perhaps, at their zenith, and when his achievement was already comparable with that of Mickiewicz or Słowacki. *Assunta* is probably the best of Norwid's narrative poems. Neither its length nor its occasional philosophical digressions are excessive or too demanding. It is a poem which is reflective without being static and emotionally rich without falling into the trap of sentimentality.

The narrative of this long poem, consisting of four cantos written in the elegant ottava rima (like Słowacki's *Beniowski*), is fairly simple. The hero-narrator goes out for a walk into the hills near the town where he lives. Here lies the monastery of the "white monks" and the wanderer gets a drink of water from them. Later on he walks into a garden to buy some flowers and strikes up a conversation with the gardener. Assunta is the gardener's granddaughter; the hero meets her and immediately falls in love with her, though she is incapable of speech. Some time later in Canto III the narrator is invited to the home of a certain Baroness; here, during tea, it transpires that the gardener met earlier is in fact employed by her and that now she is making plans to marry off Assunta to a young man of dubious reputation. This provokes the visitor's strong protest, though it is expressed in a semi-mocking conversational tone, so popular in drawing rooms, which serves to camouflage his strong involvement in the matter. The conversation is interrupted by the news that the old gardener is dying. At this point, with the poet hurrying to the gardener's bedside, the lovely Assunta turns her eyes to the sky, looking upward in silent prayer. Norwid's postscript to the poem indicates his belief that "looking to the sky" had become a theme of paintings and statues only since the time of Christ and that he attributed great importance to this "discovery."

The fourth and last canto of *Assunta* is also the most dramatic one: It relates the fulfillment of the hero's love, his happiness with Assunta which comes to an abrupt end with her sudden death. The loss of Assunta, both as a partner in love and a perfect intellectual "soul mate," is a terrible blow which cannot find adequate expression in tears or laments. He withdraws into silence, reading and rereading her letters, understanding the meaning of her words better every day. This, however, does not alleviate his "lonely suffering" which will be cured only by death—and the promise of a life after death.

In tracing the genesis of *Assunta* the biographical approach seems to be highly justified. Indeed, the poem is full of remarks and allusions that refer to Norwid's brief but serious love affair with Zofia Węgierska. In fact, the whole poem, an amalgam of an elegiac love poem with a lyrical epicedium, seems to be devoted to Węgierska's memory. This becomes a certainty with the explanation of the title: *Assunta* means "the elevated, the ascended one" in Italian (*wniebowzięta* in Polish), and this word can be directly linked to a letter of Węgierska to Norwid written shortly before her death. Here she communicated a dream in which she and Norwid sat down under a tree while he read to her something "beautiful beyond words" from a big book. The description of the dream ends with the sentence: "I was enchanted—enraptured . . ." the Polish word being *wniebowzięta* (which literally means "taken to Heaven").[20] Other allusions, such as the motif of "ivy" in Canto IV, point to the same direction—ivy was Węgierska's chosen symbol. Again, the description of historical and artistic wanderings with Assunta is a reflection and poetic summary of the many conversations between Norwid and his admiring companion who, incidentally, as correspondent of various journals and reviews in Poland often expressed views on French art and literature borrowed from the poet. Apart from these "material" proofs we may add another: the intensity of feeling in *Assunta* shows (especially in the case of such a withdrawn and philosophizing poet as Norwid) a strong emotional involvement of recent date. Since the final, ironic notes of the Kalergis affair, Norwid had lived the life of a monk, on occasion demonstrating an almost contemptuous attitude toward women. This did not exclude, however, friendly correspondence with some distant women such as Maria Trębicka or Joanna Kuczyńska. Nonetheless, his romance with Węgierska had shown his deep need for love and admiration, while the tragic outcome of the affair must have hardened his shell once again, destroying the possibility of a more "normal" and harmonious existence.

As for Assunta, she has one strange quality—her lack of speech. While it is possible that her inability to speak is the extreme symbolic realization of Norwid's theory of "meaningful silence," other possibilities could also be explored. One of these is Norwid's ideal of the "complete woman" who would embody all the original Christian virtues of goodness, simplicity, and humility. Assunta is seen and described as being close to this ideal as a woman can get: "I thought that she was an Angel, that she was my Country / The union of the Spirit with the Ideal." She can speak only with her eyes; perhaps the overall effect would be spoiled if she opened her mouth and uttered something unworthy of this idealized image. Never a poet of easy rhymes and pleasing melodies, about this time a growing *visualization* was taking place in Norwid's poetry, probably as a consequence of his hearing troubles which induced a state close to deafness.

Finally, it should be pointed out that Norwid's dumb heroine was not without precedent in nineteenth-century Polish poetry. She appeared in a long narrative poem (*Lunatyk*) by J. N. Kamiński [21] a few decades earlier bearing the name of Helena. She was rescued from a flood by the hero of the poem, but the shock that she had suffered made her lose her capacity to speak. Whereas Assunta's role in Norwid's poem is not that of a Romantic heroine of the Helena type, it is interesting to note that, as we learn from Canto III, Assunta also lost her speech "in the chaos of the flood." Knowing Norwid's preoccupation with Kamiński's linguistic theories, it is reasonable to assume that he also read Kamiński's book of poetry and that the idea of the dumb heroine impressed him (whether he realized it or not) to the point of using it himself many years later.

As in other "epic" poems by Norwid, the plot is less important than the characters' states of mind and relationships to one another. Yet *Assunta* has a dramatic and a lyrical quality at the same time. The sudden changes of light and shadow, the meaningful pauses and interruptions, all heighten the air of tension peculiar to the drama. As to the lyrical mood, it is projected both by the use of the "lyrical ego" (an unusual device in Norwid's longer poems) and by the emotional content of certain images. Though speaking in the first person enables the poet to express his feelings directly, in many instances he introduces images that express more than their lexical meaning. For one thing, *Assunta* is full of trees, plants, and herbs, symbols of the organic world which suggest either a new-fangled interest in nature or else an effort to find adequate symbols for the expression of emotional states, e.g., cypresses symbolize sadness; heliotropes—innocence and expectation. Significantly, *Assunta* begins with the metaphor of a day being flat like a paving-stone, with the poet's feeling of barrenness and "universal reification," and it opens up only slowly through following the footpath in the hills toward the monastery, becoming more and more "organic" with a succession of images: a spring, ivy, cypresses, vineyards. The first meeting between Assunta and her future lover takes place in the bower of a garden; her cottage is surrounded by ivy—and ivy will become her symbol, since in one of the last stanzas of Canto IV the narrator confesses that the sight of a branch of ivy reminds him of his dead lover. Apart from its symbolic meaning, the green world of *Assunta* seems to provide the natural background against which this idyllic and happy love affair takes place until death snatches away the most beautiful "plant"—Assunta herself.

On a nonpersonal level *Assunta* is the story of the struggle between love and fate. Fate (determinism) is seemingly stronger than love (free will), for the heroine dies; but faith (looking to the sky in anticipation of divine love) is even stronger than fate. Although others repeat the crude materialistic credo of the age: "Man is but gas, ferment, and lime" (*Człowiek jest gaz, ferment, wapno*); Norwid believes in man's being more than a handful of minerals. He believes in the immortality of the soul. Like Assunta he also looks "upwards . . . not only around." In the last and very beautiful stanza of *Assunta* Norwid speaks of his lonely suffering which will last "until one day my head will rest like an ear of corn on the sickle." [22] Here Norwid—in spite of everything, a believer—prepares himself for God's harvest. Although *Assunta* is basically a poem about love and the loss of love, it is also "a study in human loneliness, of settling the final accounts with life." [23] Its author has few illusions about the road still ahead, which will be a road of destitution and even deeper loneliness leading to the Saint Casimir Asylum.

V   From Subtle to Wild

From Norwid's last long poem *A Dorio ad Phrygium* (*From Subtle to Wild*) only a fragment of less than four hundred lines survived. The loss of this manuscript, completed around 1872, is particularly regrettable, for the existing fragment is characterized by an easy flow of narrative with sections of great poetic beauty. *A Dorio ad Phrygium* was supposed to cover a wide range of emotional states and to move presumably from the village to urban scenery in the course of its narrative. However, the tone of the surviving parts is either "subtle" or mildly ironical. This lends to the descriptive portions of the poem a certain softness of colors, somewhat unusual for Norwid, though the pastel-soft coloring is often shot through by flashes of irony. This is true even of such lyrical interludes as "O! white village dressed in the satin of the flowers of the apple-tree . . ." (which is in fact a version of the poem *Village* from the *Vade-Mecum* cycle), where the description of the Polish village is not without satirical undertones. In some respects *A Dorio ad Phrygium* reminds us of a mock-heroic epic with its invocation to the gods: "Send me the Muse, that washerwoman of manuscripts!" and its pseudo-Homeric allusions ("it happened well after the Trojan war"), though other elements of the mock-heroic epic such as the repetition of resounding epithets are absent here. The village visited and described by the poet-narrator is called *Serionice*, a pun on the words *nic* and *serio*, meaning a place where nothing is taken seriously. Although some inhabitants of the village are friendly (*Pan Salomon* or Mr. Solomon) and others charming (Rose), this "idyll of a society" which carries on its life either "beyond or beside history" raises ambivalent feelings in Norwid. This peculiar world impresses him as

> Something like the "happy islands" of the ancients
> Which has the charm of history—but not its toil or flow [24]

In this village of the "nominal kingdom" where history is neither a challenge nor an agent of change, and where politics are discussed only as much as is necessary for "respectable conversations," the poet meets an enchanting girl. The narrator contends that her beauty could be appropriately described only by a Dante, Virgil, or Hafiz and, thus, is not even attempted by the author of *A Dorio ad Phrygium*. The lyrical mood engendered by Rose's presence, on the other hand, finds its expression in an interlude which is generally considered one of the "purest" pieces of lyric ever set to paper by Norwid:

As if you throw a handful of violets
in someone's face without a word . . .

As if you rock the acacia slowly
so that its scent like dawn light
falls with white blossoms on the white
keys of the open piano . . .

As if the distant moon tangles
in the hair of one standing on the terrace
resting her brow on a luminous garland,
adorning it with silver wheat.
(Translated by Z. Bieńkowski
and Sidney S. Smith)

The charming Rose and her uncle Solomon probably played some part in the following chapters of this poetic tale, which breaks off at a point where the hero is riding through a forest at night in the company of Rose and others. Though *A Dorio ad Phrygium*, like most works of Norwid, is larded with philosophical and historico-critical generalizations, the vividness and plasticity of the characters, as well as the descriptions of nature, point to the poet's personal experience. He had, indeed, visited the Polish countryside and spent some time in manor houses both in the Congress Kingdom and in other parts of Poland. These excursions had taken place in his youth, between 1840 and 1842 and later, up to 1849. In those years he had been less critical of village life than now, when he judged the static idyll of the village in the light of history's demands and dramatic challenges. The mixed, idyllic-ironic tone of *A Dorio ad Phrygium* could hence be explained as the confrontation of two different sets of experience: the village as a place of contentment and happiness, and the village as a "backyard" of human progress.
There is one more point that warrants attention in this frag-

ment—its form. Przesmycki claimed that Norwid carried out a "basic reform in versification" in *A Dorio ad Phrygium*.[25] As this first editor and eminent critic of Norwid pointed out, Norwid began experimenting with form in a consistent manner only about 1860 while working on his unfinished tragedy *Tyrtaeus*. His efforts to make Polish verse more flexible, more suitable to contemporary themes, came to fruition in *A Dorio ad Phrygium* and in the comedy *The Ring of a Grand Lady (Pierscień Wielkiej Damy)* where his blank verse turned into completely free verse. The length of lines here alternates according to the thoughts or emotions they express, while the formal diversity of the poem is only enhanced by such rhyming lyrical interludes as the *Village* or *As If You Throw a Handful of Violets* . . . (mentioned earlier). According to Przesmycki, with his conscious application of free verse Norwid had preceded not only modern Polish but the whole of European poetry, as the French symbolists "discovered" *vers libre* only a decade or two later. While this is true and it certainly adds to Norwid's reputation as a pioneer of the new sensibility (as far as we know he never read Whitman), the fact remains that *A Dorio ad Phrygium* came to share the fate of some of Norwid's best work and was published only years after the poet's death—at a time when free verse had ceased to be a novelty and had already become part of the convention of European poetry.

CHAPTER 5

Mystery Plays and Dramas

I Zwolon

ON the Romantics' scale of values drama occupied a high
place, being regarded as the noblest form of poetry "objec-
tivized" in the conflict of historical heroes or great personalities.
Mickiewicz regarded *The Forefathers' Eve, Part III* and its
planned but never-written dramatic sequel as the most important
work of his life; Słowacki had written more than twenty plays,
and there was a period in his creative career when he wrote
poems as by-products of tragedies in verse; Krasiński is remembered chiefly for the drama *Undivine Comedy.* Norwid was less
interested in writing for the theater than his great predecessors
and rivals; his imagination was less dramatic, his historiosophy
less apocalyptic than either Słowacki's or Krasiński's. This does
not mean that he ignored the challenge of the genre, only that
as a playwright he was a late developer, his best plays being
post-Romantic rather than Romantic dramas. His first play in a
social setting, entitled *Good People* (*Dobrzy ludzie*), was lost
with the exception of a fragment. The same fate befell a historical
drama whose central hero was J. R. Patkul, a controversial seven-
teenth-century nobleman: Norwid started writing it soon after his
departure from Poland, and after a pause he resumed work on it
in 1847. We know of this lost play only from Norwid's correspondence.[1] Since his early plays anticipated Symbolist techniques,
one can only assume that Norwid's approach differed from that
of his Romantic predecessors who had also treated historical subject matter. Between 1847 and 1849 he wrote three dramatic
pieces: two mystery plays, *Wanda and Krakus*, and a strange
pseudo-drama entitled *Zwolon*. Though the latter was finished as
early as 1849 it reached the Polish reader only two years later, at
a time when the nervous excitement that had characterized the
great ideological battles and revolutionary wars of the previous

years was already subsiding and reactionary regimes were restoring "order" throughout Europe.

Zwolon was written in a different political climate and was meant for an audience still very much involved in political arguments. It has been called on occasion an "experimental play," but some critics have denied that it is a play at all and have defined it as "a monologue for many voices." Norwid himself could not make up his mind how to describe *Zwolon*, subtitling it first as a "monologue," but calling it in a letter to a friend, the poet Teofil Lenartowicz, "a dramatic sketch." This contradiction is inherent in the text which might have been conceived as a monologue, but because it could not avoid having a plot, however loosely constructed, in some ways it technically resembles a drama. *Zwolon* is an allegorical dramatic sketch, a dreamlike projection of passions and problems, written more for the "inner eye" of the mind than for the actual stage.

The title is a neologism based on an old Polish word which Norwid interpreted as "a person in harmony with God's will." Norwid's intentions in writing *Zwolon* are quite clear, thanks to the letter to Lenartowicz already mentioned in which he explained them in some detail.[2] When he moved to Paris in 1849, Norwid became passionately concerned with the difficult situation of the young émigrés of his generation, the so-called "third emigration", who had left Poland between 1844 and 1849. These young people, many of them radicals and participants in plots against the Russian or the Prussian authorities, were not greeted in France with the same enthusiasm as the refugees of 1831. They received only a minimum of material aid from the French government and lived—as a rule—from day to day, always close to starvation, which did not prevent them from getting involved in bitter political disputes. While the old emigration tried to use the newcomers for its own political ends, it was not able or prepared to give them substantial help apart from supporting such enterprises as emigration to America after 1849. Norwid called the new refugees "the most unhappy segment of Polish society" and offered the total income of *Zwolon*—this "monologue on the fate of a generation"—to the material support of his starving fellow-exiles.

Zwolon is a critique of Polish society torn by dissension and an attempt to dramatize the tragedy of the young generation out of

[86]

which one day the liberator of the future might arise. The plot, inasmuch as it exists, is not coherent at all. What is important is the clash of ideas. Despotism is opposed to the love of freedom, self-interest to "God-inspired" thought, and mass-conformism to individual conscience. Zwolon himself is not really a person, but the symbol of the thought "of an ideal Poland permeated by godliness."[3] This personified thought is stoned to death by the mindless mob after the defeat in the revolutionary war against despotism; it is later resurrected in the Child's vision and finds its final apotheosis in the triumphant entry of the Page who is also the liberator of the people. Not only Zwolon, who dies in Scene 5 to reappear as a vision in a later scene, but almost every character in this multimonologue is synthetic and symbolic: the King, Zabór, Szołom and also the Page (*Pacholę*) himself. Zabór stands for the world of despotism, Szołom for demagogy and "external, formal love," while the Page is "the young generation placed in the middle of this world bursting apart."[4] These thought-symbols are more important than the action, hence the plot is nothing but a series of monologues enlivened by brief confrontations between some of the symbols. It is therefore just to censure *Zwolon* for its lack of dramatic continuity and for the author's inconsistency in the presentation of the characters who, with the exception of the turncoat Szołom, are static and do not change throughout the play. They just keep jumping out of different boxes whenever the author wants them to appear.[5] The lack of coherence that is a salient feature of this pseudodrama is made worse by certain technical inconsistencies such as, for example, the appearance of two different "Presidents" identically named in two subsequent scenes and the confusion about the role of the youngest characters.

All this is a pity, because *Zwolon*, written as a contribution to the political and ideological debate of the late 1840's, contains some attractive lyrical passages and two or three vivid, almost dramatic scenes. One of these is Scene 3, which contains Zwolon's first confrontation with the forces of blind passion and demagogy, that is, the young romantic nationalists whose slogan reflects their wild "Wallenrodism": "Revenge, revenge on the enemy / With God, or even in spite of God!" Zwolon, and with him Norwid, rejects this program; but while Norwid put forward a positive counterprogram in his articles written at the time, and, of course, in *Promethidion,* Zwolon is incapable of putting forward anything like a cohesive counterargument: everything he does is misunderstood and misinterpreted. The voice of responsibility and caution is lost in the pandemonium of revolutionary excitement. Though his characters are symbolic, it is clear that Norwid's argument is directed against the Polish radicals of his generation. This is not to say that he is entirely on the side of the conservatives: in Scene 7 ("Night in the Vaults") where he condemns revolutionary plotting in the strongest terms, he also comes out against party politics in general. Here a heated argument develops over the question of the insignia or symbol of the clandestine movement—should it be a heart or a head? One party claims that "everything comes from the head, not from the heart," while the other faction takes up a slogan claiming exactly the opposite. The complete "love" and "unity" professed by the plotters earlier evaporates in a matter of minutes, giving way to a childish and fanatical rivalry. "Norwid . . . in Zwolon's improvisation and in the ludicrous plotters' scene, rejected in principle conspiratorial methods, the revolutionary aim, and vengeful symbols of conspiration. He set against them the myth of chivalry, which he later personified in Bem." [6] If the ironical tone of the plotters' scene recalls a similar scene in Słowacki's *Kordian,* the ending of *Zwolon* reads like a leaf taken out of *Anhelli.* The Page arrives on horseback with a mysterious army of liberators. Weak in its form and derivative in its content, *Zwolon* is more a curiosity than a living drama, though it certainly has its place in the history of Norwid's intellectual and poetic development.

II *Mystery Plays*

Norwid's two "mystery plays" *Wanda* and *Krakus* have a longer prehistory than *Zwolon,* and both are closer to the mainstream of Norwid's poetry and historiosophy than his dramatized monologue. These mystery plays were written in Rome in 1847, but their first versions have been lost. The texts printed in Norwid's *Collected Works* are the second versions of *Wanda* and of *Krakus,* both dating from 1851.

The legendary beginnings of the old Polish state were a very popular subject among Polish writers and poets in the nineteenth century. Juliusz Słowacki was not the only one who recognized the poetic potentialities of this legendary age in which he placed two of his more popular dramas *Balladyna* and *Lilla Weneda*; Kraszewski's *An Ancient Tale* (*Stara baśń*) is another effort, this time in the novel form, to evoke the atmosphere of a pre-Christian and proto-Polish Slavic community. Zygmunt Krasiński was also interested in this period—witness his dramatic fragment *Wanda*. All of them benefited from the results of the extensive historical research on pre-Christian Poland which was, to some extent, a corollary to the rise of romantic nationalism. Norwid was particularly conscientious in the exploitation of his sources, which probably included Długosz's chronicle and Lukasz Gołębiowski's book on Polish folk-customs and superstitions. His two mystery plays dramatizing the most popular legends of Polish prehistory (Krak, or Krakus, the dragon-killer founder of Cracow, and Queen Wanda who killed herself because "she did not want to marry a German") were different from the typical products of the Romantic theater. They underemphasized both passion and violence; they treated the heroes of the legend with a most un-Romantic religious reverence.

These plays can be called mystery plays on account of the symbolic character and almost hieratic behavior of the main protagonists. Norwid, of course, interprets the legend in an idiosyncratic way. For him Wanda's sacrifice is not so much an act of nationalistic or patriotic defiance of the Germans as a voluntary act of love toward her people and, judging from her speech in Scene 6, a kind of *imitatio Christi*. In other words, Norwid interprets Wanda as a precursor of Christianity. In fact, the time of her death is supposed to fall on Good Friday A.D. 33. Having seen a vision of Christ, she realizes that she has to lay down her life for her people. In *Krakus* Norwid creates a genuinely dramatic situation by introducing two brothers, Rakuz and Krakus, whose conflict ends with Rakuz's fratricide. Here Rakuz is the symbol of power-seeking pride, while Krakus stands for a humble, self-sacrificing (hence "Christian") courage.

Wanda contains some vaguely beautiful lyrical passages, but the plot is too thin and, in the last analysis, undramatic. Perhaps Kraszewski was right in saying that though many poets had attempted to write on Wanda "bringing this ethereal shape down to earth, this inadvertently diminishes and destroys the charm which she has in folk stories." [7] The best part of *Wanda* is probably Scene 6 in which choirs of women, children, and various craftsmen mourn the young Queen in sad, majestic hexameters. The same chanting crowd of pre-Christian Slavs, slowly approaching, appears in Norwid's lyric masterpiece *The Funeral Rhapsody in Bem's Memory*, which was written at approximately the same time; the poem on Bem is also in hexameters.

Krakus has a more intricate plot, more dramatic movement and more genuine mystery than *Wanda*. Although based on the story of the lengendary hero who slew the fearful dragon (a common enough motif in folktales throughout Europe), the conflict between the two brothers, both set on killing the dragon, constitutes the core of the play. While Rakuz prevaricates and enacts the dragon-killing only in a dream-fantasy, Krakus arrives in disguise and kills the monster. After his victory Rakuz, the ruling prince, asks "the unknown knight" to reveal his identity. When Krakus is unwilling to do so, he is challenged to a fight in the course of which he is killed by his brother for "showing contempt to the people." This is Rakuz's own interpretation. As for the people, they are still crying out for Krakus with the words: "Where is our savior?" Rakuz replies in a sentence which dramatically sums up the essence of the situation, reflecting the false logic of power: "The savior?—he who rules!" The people, whatever their outward behavior, cannot accept this. They honor the impersonal sacrifice of the hooded knight by burning his remains at night and by raising a burial mound to him. His name is still unknown to the people, but his sacrifice is not forgotten.

The central character of the play, Prince Krakus goes a long way in developing his potentialities. In the first two scenes he is still a lonely, depressed introvert; he is rejected and forsaken by his brother and doubts the sense of his mission. Then, as in a fairy tale, he enters the enchanted forest and in Scene 4 is addressed by the magic Threshold. Still hesitant, he crosses it—this is equivalent to the symbolic acceptance of his mission. During the night he is initiated by the Spring and prepared for the great task of dragon-killing. Fortified with an Orpheus-like poetic skill (he sings a song before entering the dragon's cave), he slays the dragon. Would he be less of a hero if he showed his face to the crowd? Why does he refuse? One possibility is that he does not want to become king, replacing his brother Rakuz whom he still loves and respects. Another is that the nature of his initiation is such that after he has accomplished his task he is not supposed to speak. He is another Quidam—his deeds speak for him; he will not defend them.

The significance of *Krakus* is twofold. First, the legend is transformed into a mystery play in such a way that its symbolic, rather than romantic or naturalistic, aspects are stressed. This prepares the way for the truly symbolic theater of Wyspiański almost half a century later. Second, the hero is not only archetypal but also "popular": there is a deep sense of community between Krakus and his people. Though fighting "evil" on a higher level, the Prince's fight with the dragon is not an isolated moral gesture. It is done for the people; it has a liberating effect on their life. Krakus is a personification of the ideal hero as seen in Norwid's "populist," that is, basically pre-*Promethidion*, period, although his self-chosen anonymity already gives a foretaste of the hero-concept developed fully after 1851, a concept not identical but in some ways similar to that of "organic work."

III   *Social Comedies before 1872*

Norwid's work as a dramatist includes a number of dramatic miniatures of no great consequence. Of these only *The One Thousand and Second Night* (*Noc tysiączna druga*, 1850) deserves separate notice for its light, ironical, almost Mussetian treatment of a poet's disappointed love for a lady of high social standing. This one-act comedy, which takes place in a small Italian town near Verona, already raises one of the central problems of Norwid's later plays: the rejection of the artist by the salon, personified here by the Lady "surrounded by . . . a glitter of formalism."

Three plays, and the fragment *Countess Palmyra* written between 1861 and 1872 were in fact "true comedies," comprising not only comic incidents from everyday life or conflicts between different social conventions but also individual conflicts which express the hidden essence of social relations. When reporting the completion of *The Ring of a Grand Lady* to a friend, Norwid deliberately used the term *haute comédie,* adding that no such term exists in Polish for "[our] society has never looked at itself with its own eyes." [8] This statement implies, and the texts bear it out, that although the author lived in France, his social plays or true comedies reflect above all Polish society, even if there are two kinds of Polish societies observed and blended in these plays—a patriarchal and a modern one. In fact, as Wyka pointed out, in Norwid's plays there are parallels with the kind of problems raised by some Polish Positivists after 1864.

Of *The Actor* (*Aktor*), the first of these plays, only the draft version survived; this circumstance might explain some of its structural weaknesses. The main protagonists of the play are young Count George, the owner of Sphinx Castle, and his friend, an actor with the somewhat bizarre name Gotard Pszonk-kin. Due to the sudden bankruptcy of the Viennese firm Glückschnell and Co. where he had invested large sums, the Count finds himself penniless with an aging mother and a young sister to support. After some hesitation he takes up Gotard's offer and becomes a professional actor. As he is not the only one whom the fall of the Glückschnell has ruined (Glückschnell is an expressive name, it could be freely rendered as Quickbuck), Norwid has an opportunity to describe the ways in which other members of Count George's class adapt themselves to the new situation. Prince Philemon, for example, marries the rich widow of a wine merchant; young Erasmus, who backs out of his obligation to marry George's sister Elisa, is to marry the daughter of the restaurant-owner Mr. Bizoński. Adaptation is the password of this "industrial, commercial age" with its unscrupulous entrepreneurs, vulgar but industrious manufacturers, impoverished aristocrats, and lonely, impecunious, but proud artists. Norwid despises the moral atmosphere of rational calculation around him in which economic interests are the visible or hidden mainspring of almost every action and he denounces a society which seems to him to be dehumanized by the impersonal power of money. As Elisa puts it: "Indeed, people are like automatons / Whom something pulls by a string from behind the scenes." [9] Individual relations in *The Actor* are theatrical or false: Count George has to playact while hiding from his family the extent of their financial catastrophe; Gotard has to act the part of a visiting businessman for Elisa and his friend's mother to hide his "socially unacceptable" occupation; Erasmus turns out to be a part-time actor in real life, as he keeps hopping from engagement to engagement. Count George finally becomes a real actor, and this reveals Norwid's "message" which could be axiomatically formulated as follows: it is much preferable to be an authentic actor (an artist) than a puppet of economic necessity or an actor "without con-

viction" (forced into an unwanted or anachronistic social role).
Count George's choice is the right one. Although his mother is
first shocked by the loss of social standing involved in her son's
change of profession, at the end of the play (which Gomulicki
restored to *Selected Writings* on the basis of the first draft), she
forgives him when she realizes that he became an actor to pay
his debts and to save the good name of the family.

The structure of *The Actor* is somewhat muddled, and the plot
is not too coherent. Norwid brings too many characters onto the
stage, and some scenes are only loosely connected. Moments of
dramatic tension are few and far between, but at least *The Actor*
has three finished acts and an epilogue (dubbed somewhat
strangely an "epode"), an important advantage over his next
"true comedy" *Behind the Scenes: Tyrtaeus* (*Za kulisami: Tyrtej*).
The significance of *The Actor* lies not so much in its formal aspects as in its incisive commentary on the state of society caught
up in the process of *embourgeoisement*. The central problem of
The Actor is really "the birth of the Polish intelligentsia." [10] Even
if cases like that of Count George were relatively rare, the fact
that Norwid chose this subject shows his preoccupation with the
problem and that he did not regard Count George's choice as
humiliating. Gotard and the Count are intellectual equals and they
are both worthy of respect; if anyone, it is the so-called "practical
men" who deserve our contempt. Erasmus is one of these and
Norwid puts into his mouth the ironic condemnation of the
"romantics":

> . . . The present epoch
> Is serious . . . it is not an Epoch of romances
> But of administration, of order. If it is colder
> Than it used to be, so have a fur-coat . . .[11]

Norwid does not like romantic extremes, but he has even less
sympathy for a character like the one quoted above; this is clear
from the advice "have a fur-coat" where irony changes into
cynicism. Choosing Count George for his main hero does not
mean that the fate of the Polish aristocracy concerned Norwid
deeply; he was more interested in the psychological process of
adaptation. The industrial age forces this adaptation on most
individuals but each choice involves a drama. The representative

individual when confronted with this choice finds himself in a truly "Hamletic" situation. This is why Count George's personal drama is in fact bound up with Shakespeare's *Hamlet*. In Act 1 we are told that once in Edinburgh he played Hamlet at an amateur performance; in Act 3 while waiting for Gotard at the railway station, he actually reads aloud Hamlet's monologue. The "Epode" informs us about his first appearance on the stage when he played Hamlet instead of Gotard Pszonk-kin. Given the Count's high moral principles, the only other choice in his situation would have been suicide. The chance given him by his friend saves both his self-respect and his life. There is, nevertheless, much irony in Norwid's solution. To be authentic in this age one has to become an actor who grows up to his role. Nonetheless, even the best actor (or artist) will be denounced by people of the age, by "serious" people of Erasmus's ilk who claim that "acting is . . . an eloquent school of deception."

Behind the Scenes (written in 1865–66, the last draft being dated from 1869) has a much more complicated structure than *The Actor*. It consists of a prologue in prose, a prologue in verse, a poem dedicated to Warsaw, a prose introduction, and two plays linked together, both interspersed by lyrical interludes. The verse prologue (*W pamiętniku*) describes in a somewhat Dantesque manner the Traveler's experiences in hell where there are "no brothers, neighbors or people / only *studies* on the heart of brothers!" Also there are "no feelings, only motives" and "no aims, only routine." [12] This place, as we might well expect, is contemporary society. As it is only loosely connected with the play the verse prologue is often printed separately and by a curious turn of fate two stanzas of this poem made Norwid's name widely known among non-Polish speakers for the first time: they were quoted in Andrzej Wajda's excellent film *Ashes and Diamonds*. In fact, the title of the film (and of Jerzy Andrzejewski's novel) is taken from Norwid's rhetorical question—whether from one's whole life nothing else will remain but ashes, or could it be that these ashes hide a "radiant diamond"?

The play itself, subtitled by Norwid "a fantasy," takes place not so much in Hell as in a sort of limbo, in the vestibule of a theater. We witness—first indirectly from the comments and remarks of the audience and later as a play within the play—the first performance of Count Omegitt's drama *Tyrtaeus*. Omegitt's play

Mystery Plays and Dramas

is a failure; at least it fails to please the audience. As a result, Lia breaks her engagement with the Count, ostentatiously returning his ring, and plans to eventually marry Sofistoff, a high government official. He is a Russian, albeit a very cosmopolitan and sophisticated gentleman (as his name indicates) with a special interest in the theater.[13] Lia is shown as the typical product of her social class. Above all the false norms and expectations of Polish society are condemned through her character. In the vestibule of the theater the entire Warsaw "high society" of the 1860's is present, though more as "types" and masques than real persons. Omegitt's play is produced at Carnival time which affords Norwid the opportunity to bring masques onto the stage; these "dominoes" and "violets" are in fact plotters, police agents, and actors in disguise.

As for Omegitt's rivals and enemies there are Sofistoff, Glück-schnell, and Fiffraque, the successful French playwright. Glück-schnell appears here not as a banker but as a friend, indeed, a patron of "the arts," by which he means easily digestible entertainment. He is a great consumer of vaudevilles and comedies and finds Omegitt's ideas and language strange and hard to accept. *Behind the Scenes* amounts to a declaration of faith by Norwid: good poetry, authentic art simply *cannot be popular* as long as fashion or economic interests have priority over truth; it will inevitably clash with the representatives of such interests and will be rejected by them. Authentic art, as Norwid had asserted many times, has to serve truth without regard to the consequences. False art can appear masked in different ways. Irena Sławińska, a Norwid critic, lists some of these as being implicitly criticized in *Behind the Scenes*. Inauthentic art can be the melodrama or light entertainment demanded by Glückschnell, the "national tendentiousness" in art hailed by one of the Dominoes, or else the primitive rhymes and jingling doggerel of the "popular poet."[14] Norwid, through his alter ego Omegitt, rejects all these and gives expression to his deep-seated skepticism about contemporary society which is ultimately a reflection of the civilization that had produced it. In Omegitt's view "European civilization is a bastard" because "all those who are *practically intelligent* are not Christian and all who are *Christian* are impractical!"[15] The word "Christian" does not necessarily mean religious allegiance here; rather it is synonymous with "conscien-

tious" or "truthful" or "filled with love for one's fellowmen"—
which the age of triumphant industrialism certainly was not,
either in France or in Poland.

Behind the Scenes is interesting and valuable both as a poetic
and an unusual, almost twentieth-century, dramatic text, but it
is likely to confront the theatrical director with difficult problems. It is after all an incomplete diptych of a play, and even the
link between the two parts *Behind the Scenes* and *Tyrtaeus* is
tenuous enough. Conceiveably, imaginative staging could make
up for the fragmentariness of the text. Among the "true comedies"
only one is really coherent and written with special regard for
the nature of the theater—*The Ring of a Grand Lady* (*Pierścień
Wielkiej Damy*). Norwid wrote it for a drama competition in
Cracow in 1872, though it was at the time completely ignored by
the jury. Its rediscovery and repeated staging since the 1930's
have made it the most popular of his plays.

IV   The Ring of a Grand Lady

The Ring of a Grand Lady continues on a higher level the
Omegitt theme of the social isolation and humiliation of the
artist. Its main hero, Mac X, or as the Polish text "translates" his
name, *Mak-Yks*, is a young poet like Omegitt, but without comparable social rank. He is a penniless intellectual living in a house
of Countess Maria Harrys, the widow of a relative of Mac X. The
Countess practices charity by allowing the poet to live in the
house without realizing that Mac X is secretly in love with her.
Not that such a realization would matter to her. There is a vast
social, and also a psychological, gap between the two. The
Countess professes no interest in "earthly love" which she sees
as fickle and unstable; she prefers to attend church regularly
and to fulfill her social "duties." Cold and beautiful in a detached,
self-encasing way she is very much the Grand Lady of the
Second Empire salons, Norwid's female archetype, constant
temptress and tormentor. What is extraordinary about the Countess is perhaps the basic instability of her position—only this
enables her to act in the way she does in a moment of truth,
offering, in an outburst of generosity, her hand to the man who
truly loves her. All the same, it is difficult to forget that the
Countess had earlier (Act 2, Scene 1) in an offhand remark divided mankind into two categories: people and "nonpeople."

Mystery Plays and Dramas

Servants, for example, are nonpeople. One can get quietly dressed in front of them—they just do not count. This gives Mac X, the poor relative and himself a nonperson, a chance to reflect on the possibility of "nonpersons" becoming the only *real* persons in certain moments or situations. This argument expresses both the paradoxical nature of Mac X's own situation (he knows that his talent and human qualities are superior to those approved by salon conventions) and the "unreality" of the Countess's life—it is only at the end of the play that she gains the opportunity of a more authentic existence. At any rate, the finality of the happy ending is rather doubtful; the marriage between the Countess and Mac X only opens up a very ambiguous perspective. As Jan Kott says: "This 'white tragedy' is in reality a comedy of Romantic gestures in the real world of bourgeois prose." [16]

The Ring of a Grand Lady, though written for the theater, bristles with philosophical passages and highly poetic metaphors. Apart from Mac X, Count Szeliga is another character who utters poetically formulated truths. Initially a suitor of Countess Maria, his attentions in the course of the play are transferred to Magdalene, the Countess' confidante. He is a traveler, a philosopher, and an astronomer, the only person who is ready to give practical help to Mac X in the form of an offer of a free boat ticket to the United States. He, Magdalene, and the old servant Salome (whose "diamond words" Szeliga notes with admiration) are in addition to Mac X the positive characters in the play, whereas Durejko, an ex-judge and the Countess's factotum, and his wife represent an obdurate philistinism posing as "practicality." Events certainly would not take the turn they do were it not for Durejko. When in Act 3 the diamond ring of the Countess is lost, Durejko calls the police. Thus, indirectly, he is responsible for the happy ending. Consequently, he congratulates himself in the last scene: "For who brought this about? . . . who?—if you please —became the first *cause* . . . ," describing his role as "Durejko *ex-machina*." It would be difficult to find a more ironical ending to this comedy rich in ironical nuances and undertones.

Although there are similarities between the concept of Alfred de Vigny's play *Chatterton* and Norwid's best comedy, in the latter the autobiographical element is strong as well. The Countess is modeled on Maria Kalergis (even the names sound similar: Harrys-Kalergis), the celebrated "grand dame" of Paris society;

Magadalene on her friend Maria Trębicka with whom Norwid had corresponded for many years. In a sense Norwid's last humiliation by Kalergis, the real circumstances of which are unknown, is dramatized in the incident with the diamond ring and it is revenged symbolically. In the play the Countess realizes the meanness of her behavior toward Mac X and offers to marry him, partly as an act of repentance. Nevertheless, we have seen enough of her earlier to doubt the permanence of this arrangement. The Countess is too much a slave to the conventions of her class to become the ideal wife of whom Mac X had been dreaming. It is ironic, moreover, that Mac X is in love with *her* and not with the much more human and warm-hearted Magdalene, but then he sees Countess Harrys through his illusions. Mac X's situation is truly paradoxical. In the first act he is on the verge of suicide. He has been thrown out of his room and he is literally starving. This is why at the party of the Countess he hides a piece of bread in his pocket. The incident of the ring curiously contrasts with his predicament; a remark made by Szeliga in Act I compares talents to diamonds, pointing out that those hiding in the earth are not less valuable than the finished product "accidentally fallen out of a ring." Real talent, in the spirit of this simile, can be likened to an unpolished diamond which still "lives" in its natural habitat, while the polished diamond set in a ring is but "dead jewelry," reflecting conventional values only.

While the psychological makeup of the characters in *The Ring of a Grand Lady* is colored by Romantic elements, the play itself transcends the Romantic tradition. In fact, the structure of the play keeps the classic principle of the unities. There is one change of scene from the house where Mac X and Szeliga live to the Harrys's Villa not far away, but the plot is fitted into a day, starting in the morning and ending in the early evening. Each act takes place at a different time of the day which means that Norwid subordinates dramatic time to the rhythm of time set by the convention of the salon.[17] The drama is written in blank verse which could, of course, convey Romantic content, but in this case it proves to be an admirably flexible form in which all the modes of speech used by Norwid fit without difficulty. Some of the characters, like Mac X himself, speak in a poetic mode often resorting to elliptic speech; their *true* pathos is contrasted with the *false* pathos and the pragmatic lapidary quality characterizing the speech of others like Mr. and Mrs. Durejko, the guests at the party, and occasionally the Countess. Ironic implications also appear in the text of both positive and negative characters; in the case of the positive ones their relationship to "true pathos" is the same as that of the pragmatic lapidary quality to "false pathos"—they complement each other. Although some times, for example, in the speech of old Salome, the caretaker, Norwid introduces colloquial expressions, even his simple characters speak poetry sooner or later:

> Oh my God!
> The world is loath to have its quiet people:
> As in a flood, they are carried farther
> And farther away, constantly pushed by the waves
> Until one day they are swept under. . . .[18]

At the same time Norwid's "white tragedy" has certain realistic traits. Although the surroundings are cosmopolitan and some of the names (Mac X, Harrys) foreign-sounding, the social milieu is definitely Polish and mid-nineteenth century. The only thing we are told about the setting is that the play "takes place in the Harrys's Villa and in its vicinity." Among the characters there are such different types as Mr. Durejko, the pedantic "graduate of Dorpat Academy" who intersperses his utterances with Latin quotations and with clumsy and weird neologisms (aping the Polish Romantic philosopher and political writer Trentowski), and Szeliga, the enlightened and much-traveled Count who "wears a beard and has even visited Jerusalem." Their first encounter produces a genuinely comic and highly realistic situation. Another scene which strikes the reader with its realism is in the third act where Mrs. Durejko reprimands Mac X, who instead of joining in a parlor game sits alone eating cakes. She has no way of knowing that Mac X had not eaten since morning.

The Ring of a Grand Lady takes place against the social backdrop of the salon, and this circumstance lends the play a certain character of intimacy. It is played in a small circle where each person's social role and duties are exactly circumscribed, though there is some room for "eccentric" or "Romantic" behavior. In staging it every detail warrants special attention: intonation, mime, gestures. In fact, the text is conspicuously full of the author's instructions as to the manner of speaking certain lines (seriously, slowly, jokingly, etc.) as well as indicating movements, gestures, even facial expressions. This "true comedy," Norwid's best, is altogether rich in fine psychological observations and in dramatic nuances. While it did not influence the development of Polish comedy in the last quarter of the nineteenth century, it is certainly not inferior to the plays of more successful authors of the same period such as Tadeusz Rittner or Gabriela Zapolska.

V Cleopatra and Caesar

In a letter to Józef Bohdan Zaleski dated November, 1872, Norwid informed his friend about the successful completion of *The Ring of a Grand Lady* and added: "Half of the third act of my beloved tragedy which, after Shakespeare, I have hesitated to write for a long time, is still missing: [it is] *Cleopatra and Caesar* in three acts." [19] The task which the poet had set himself was very ambitious, and we can assume that he was not quite happy with the first results. Six years later he rewrote the whole play, but even then failed to complete it. The large surviving fragment of the tragedy, which breaks off in the middle of Act 3, was not published until many years after Norwid's death.

As Norwid expressly said in the letter quoted above, *Cleopatra and Caesar* (*Kleopatra i Cezar*) was written "for the stage, in accordance with the technical requirements of the theater." Whatever efforts Norwid made to meet these requirements, the play still reads more like a *Lesedrama*, a dramatic poem structured into dialogues. Before writing his tragedy Norwid had studied the historical background thoroughly, at one point even attempting to learn how to decipher Egyptian hieroglyphs. He knew his Plutarch well and read other authors relevant to his theme. Steeped in Egyptian cultural history and in his studies of Roman beliefs and customs, Norwid was well equipped to draw a convincing background to *Cleopatra and Caesar*; unfortunately, the plot itself lacks excitement and dramatic tension. Above all, it lacks Shakespeare's sense of timing and sense of humor. Monumental and dignified, Norwid's tragedy was said by a modern critic to be "static as a statue . . . it is the statue of thought." [20] Whatever function this lack of dynamism may have in setting the mood of the play, it is by definition antitheatrical.

Although the main heroes of the tragedy are Julius Caesar and Cleopatra, Norwid allows only one great confrontation between the two and even on that occasion they discuss Rome and Egypt in historiosophic terms (Act 1, Scene 6). Again, in the third act when Cleopatra is expecting Marc Antony's arrival, instead of considering her own fate or possible relationship with the victorious Roman, she breaks into a monologue about Rome's decline and the contradiction between its greatness and the basic antihumanism underlying this greatness ("Rome is great . . . but that greatness cannot stand *man* on its own!"). In other words, Norwid seems more preoccupied with the historical tragedy of the Roman Empire and of the Ptolemaic kingdom built on Egypt's ancient culture than with the individual tragedy of Cleopatra torn between conflicting passions and contradictory allegiances. Norwid's Cleopatra is too subtle, too much of a lonely thinker, an introvert, and his Caesar, impeccably noble and eloquent, is an idealized hero, a representative of traditional Roman virtues. Once they understand each other in "historiosophic" terms, there is no obstacle in the way of their love. Though they represent two entirely different cultures their love affair is not problematical, offering no dramatic conflicts or clashes.

Even if it is difficult to admire *Cleopatra and Caesar* as a tragedy, it can be admired for the plasticity of its language and for the occasional poetic image or metaphor that lights up its dialogues and monologues. The Knight's monologue in Act 2 includes a description of "the symphony of the night," all the diverse and often minute noises that fill the cool and moist Egyptian night, which is a lyric masterpiece. Once again Norwid uses thirteen-syllable blank verse with great virtuosity to express philosophical reflections, ordinary conversations, and sudden emotional outbursts with almost equal ease. *Cleopatra and Caesar* is not without interest for the cultural historian or for the student of ideas. The values of different civilizations, of past-oriented Egypt and present-conscious Rome clash here on a symbolic level with the future tragedy of the protagonists intimated in the terrible prophecy of Szechera, the seer. Occasionally, Norwid's Egyptians appear to show some similarity with Slavs and his Romans with Western Europeans. When Norwid contrasts the Egyptians' passive indolence and hollow pride with the serious, active, and practical stance of Caesar and of the Romans, the comparison might be driving home a point. Caesar's death, lamented by Cleopatra in the third act, is interpreted as the end of an epoch.

It marks the beginnings of Christianity, a religion which will make up for Rome's lack of compassion for non-Romans and for its disregard of individual dignity. Cleopatra's loneliness also has wider implications, reflecting the loneliness of mankind in the historical gap between two great epochs, two great religious and cultural formations. Cleopatra knows intuitively that the coming era will express those ideas which were left unexpressed by her own epoch: "Man is an infant / of things not yet put into words!" [21] This thought was to be taken up and developed later in Norwid's last and important essay, *Silence.*

CHAPTER 6

Norwid's Prose

1 Flowers for the Dead

NORWID'S prose works can be, by and large, divided into two groups, that of narrative and that of discursive prose. Even if the latter plays a not unimportant part in showing Norwid's intellectual and literary development with some essays and prose introductions providing a valuable background to Norwid's poetic practice, his achievement in narrative prose will be discussed first. His entire output as a writer of fiction would fill only a slim volume consisting of ten stories. While four of these—openly, or in a thinly disguised form—have some autobiographical relevance and include personal reminiscences, three are "legends" or parables, and only the last three, the so-called "Italian" stories can be classified as short stories proper.

The Kind Guardian, or Bartholomew Becomes Alphonse (*Łaskawy opiekun czyli Bartłomiej Alfonsem*), Norwid's first piece of narrative prose, was written as early as 1840. It is a very simple story, telling, in some detail, of the life and circumstances of a young boy who has lost his parents and now lives in the house of his guardian, a self-styled Colonel, in the country. Young Bartholomew is constantly slighted and cold-shouldered by his guardian's family and feels unwanted in this house where he has to feign gratitude for his very modest upkeep. Eventually, the Colonel comes upon a document revealing that Bartholomew is in fact of noble blood and was originally called Alphonse. This gives him the pretext to get rid of the boy by pretending that his country house is "not good enough" for a person of such high social standing. While the characters are not particularly original and the plot is unsophisticated, the story written in a humorous vein with glimpses of sharp irony is quite readable. Although based on Norwid's own youthful experiences, as a picture of a young orphan's tribulations *The Kind Guardian* is not sufficiently dramatic. However, it comes off reasonably well as social satire illustrating, among other things, the particular pretensions and general ignorance of the landed gentry, as well as the sheer boredom of provincial drawing-room conversations. This realistic sketch shows more affinity with Kraszewski's early stories than with the then fashionable *gawęda* with its colorful and long-winded personal reminiscences of notable events or with Romantic tales of the past.[1]

There is less social reality and considerably more symbolic import in Norwid's next tale *Dominic* (*Menego*). This very brief story, written in 1850 and subtitled *Fragment from a Diary*, is told in the first person singular and relates a peculiar experience that befell Norwid in Venice soon after his first arrival in Italy. Here he kept meeting Tytus Byczkowski, a Polish painter many years his senior. They would often sit in a cheap coffeehouse sipping coffee, discussing Venetian architecture or esthetics. One day two casual, seemingly insignificant, conversations take place. First Byczkowski describes the latest picture on which he has started working. It represents a fisherman showing his children the catch of the day—no fish, nothing, but an empty shell. After this episode the Polish painter calls the waiter but instead of saying "Domenico" or "Menego" (a more colloquial form of "Dominic"), he puts the stress in the characteristic Polish manner on the penultimate syllable, exclaiming: *"me-négo"* ("I am drowning"). The waiter finds this funny and cracks a joke about the coffeehouse being quite dry. Next day Byczkowski sends a farewell letter and a souvenir to Norwid, and the same day he commits suicide by swimming out into the sea. "His grave is at the Lido," writes Norwid in conclusion to this short but moving story, where small and insignificant-looking details gain dramatic significance in the light of later events. For instance, the meaning of Byczkowski's last picture suddenly becomes clear: it is the symbolic expression of his fear of being a failure. The waiter's mispronounced name, on the other hand, projects the artist's mode of death.

If *Dominic* is more than a mere anecdote because of the symbolic anticipation of the painter's tragedy, *Black Flowers* (*Czarne kwiaty*), Norwid's most popular prose piece, is of an even wider interest, though not entirely for the same reason. It is also about the circumstances of death and farewell, but of people better-known than Byczkowski: the poet Witwicki, Chopin, Słowacki, Mickiewicz, and the French painter Delaroche. It is also a kind of excerpt from the poet's diary, written in a discreetly poetic, somewhat impressionistic style. Norwid confesses in the first passage of *Black Flowers* that he intends to avoid having a "style" altogether, the absence of a conspicuous style being a sign of respect for his subject matter. He aims at nothing more than taking "daguerreotypes" of certain people whom he met shortly before their death. Witwicki, a minor poet who lived and died in Italy, is remembered as uttering strange words in a bout of fever talking about some flowers which only he could see. Norwid, arguably, calls his sketch *Black Flowers* for the same reason: he alone can recall exactly *these* memories, no one else has noticed these "flowers." His reminiscences include factual information on each person, descriptions of personal habits, living circumstances, and snippets of conversation that have taken place between Norwid and the person remembered. Certain phrases or sentences stick out as having a special significance. In the case of Chopin, whom Norwid visited in his flat in the Rue Chaillot, the ailing composer's remark, interrupted by a fit of coughing, is misunderstood by Norwid in such a way as to intimate Chopin's impending death. Słowacki himself tells Norwid that he is going to die soon, whereas while parting from Mickiewicz the unusual tone of the older poet's good-bye (and possibly its literal meaning: *à Dieu*—with God!) becomes a portent of his fate, his death in Constantinople.[2] Though some of Norwid's observations show great perception and accuracy (the "completeness" of Chopin's gestures, the old-fashioned way in which Mickiewicz is dressed), it is not so much their documentary value that makes these sketches memorable, but the carefully modulated tone and artistic sensitivity with which Norwid evokes the shadows of people who had been close to him for one reason or another. The language of *Black Flowers* is dignified but supple; it is also poetic, especially in its combinations of adjectives ("Seraphic-bloody," "deep-amaranth-sapphire-colored") and the long, melancholic sentences remind one of a nocturne played on the piano.

White Flowers (*Białe kwiaty*), written in 1859, differs from its "black" counterpart by being much more of an essay illustrated by anecdotes than an account of experiences concerning outstanding personalities. The word "white" in the title indicates the main

object of Norwid's reflections, which is silence. The author of
Vade-Mecum perceives silence as a dramatic substance and claims
that the most poetic moments in Schiller's dramas are those when
the actors keep completely silent. He goes on to discuss a wide
range of different "silences," such as the "blue and festive" silence
of an evening spent by the Castel Gandolfo near Albano, the
stunned and frightening silence during a performance of *Macbeth*
in Rome soon after the assassination of Minister Rossi, and the
infinitely deep silence of the wintry ocean experienced during his
passage to America. *White Flowers* is, in fact, an interesting sequel to the young poet's speculation on silence. Furthermore, it
has points of connection with the essay *Silence* in which Norwid
many years later was to expound his esthetic theory about the
central function of silence (or rather *przemilczenie*, already referred to earlier) in art. Because of its discussion of theoretical
questions, *White Flowers* is written in a more idiosyncratic and
more difficult style than its "black" counterpart. The two pieces,
though independent of each other, are linked by one episode:
by conversations with a young Jewish immigrant during the
passage to the New World. In *Black Flowers* this is evoked in
connection with the sudden death of the beautiful Irishwoman
whom both passengers had noticed, while the episode relating to
"all those Sundays" spent on the boat in *White Flowers* can be
read as a continuation of the same story. Within *White Flowers*
the different episodes told by Norwid have no logical connection;
what holds them together is a certain mood deriving from the
dramatic character of silence.

II   *Norwid's "Legends"*

Both *Black Flowers* and *White Flowers* were personal confes-
sions of a man with a rare gift for minute observations and with
a deep faith in Providence and in individual destiny. The book
that Norwid held in the highest regard at the time was the Bible.
Small wonder that in his later prose works he tried to emulate
the parable style of the Scriptures, this ambition being most apparent in *The Last Tale* (*Ostatnia z bajek*). Also, for many years,
he wrote no other fiction than "legends." Of these *The Bracelet*
(*Bransoletka*) is the closest to an anecdote which was, perhaps,
the reason why Norwid gave it the subtitle *A Legend from the
Nineteenth Century*. At first reading *The Bracelet* appears to be

a somewhat meager story. The narrator is introduced at a ball to a certain Eulalia, a very attractive and fashionable lady (in Norwid's vocabulary "fashionable" has distinctly unpleasant connotations). He then leaves the ball and finds a bracelet in the street. This turns out to be Edgar's engagement present to Eulalia, which the narrator, not knowing to whom this valuable object belongs, gives to a poor ragpicker, who is to find the owner and collect a reward for it. Later the narrator's poet-friend brings the news of the engagement being broken, the story ending with an ironic postscript: "Eulalia married the Banker and they are happy." The moral of the story, or rather its message, is Norwid's conviction that his epoch abuses the sacrament of marriage; but in order to drive home this point he could have used the device of irony less discreetly.

More striking and more relevant to the overall picture of the epoch is another "legend," entitled *Civilization* (*Cywilizacja*). Here again Norwid's own experiences provide the background to the story of a voyage across the Atlantic, though neither the Romantic beginning of the tale nor its realistic details can overshadow its basically symbolic character. The steamer *Civilization* is a microcosm of society. It symbolizes the whole of Western civilization in the middle of the nineteenth century, not unlike Melville's river-steamer in *The Confidence Man.* The passengers aboard have no specific names, and are types rather than individuals: the Cavalry officer, the Captain, the Conspirator, the Editor, the Missionary, and the Archaeologist. There is also an Interpreter who looks after a group of "wild ambassadors . . . from some far-away island." Repeatedly it is pointed out how impressed these men are by *Civilization*—especially when she is sailing in fine weather. Norwid's hero, on the other hand, is not much impressed by the boat and is even less impressed by his fellow-passengers. He feels lonely and cannot see in what way they can alleviate his loneliness. From fine weather the steamboat sails into a storm. Still later she is caught between floating icebergs and a catastrophe seems imminent. In this critical situation the morale of the crew and of the passengers quickly crumbles. Nonetheless they will not face up to the crisis. When the Missionary asks the Captain to inform everyone about the seriousness of the situation, he is opposed by the Captain and others so as "not to create panic." Finally, a fire breaks out and the ship gets wrecked. We are not certain about the narrator's fate, whether in the last short chapter of the story he is still alive or whether what he sees is a vision after death. As for the *Civilization*, she is finished.

While Norwid might have borrowed the idea of representing industrial civilization as a steamboat from Victor Hugo in whose poem *Plein Mer, Plein Ciel* (1859) the fate of a gigantic steamboat, the *Leviathan*, is likened to that of "this epoch" or civilization,[3] his symbolic judgment of the age expressed in this tale is in fact the result of his personal experiences and reflections on the state of affairs in Western society. *Civilization* shows Norwid's growing awareness of the vulnerability of the industrial civilization which is disguised by a constant display of self-righteousness by the spokesmen of society and is increased by their quasi-religious awe and enthusiasm for technological progress. While he did not spare this "trading and industrial" epoch in his poems, in his cautionary tale he went further, foreseeing the icebergs of history which sooner or later would shatter the convenient myth of progress. The long-flowing sentences of the story and the very art form used indicate that the time factor is relatively unimportant. Norwid does not think in years or decades but in epochs. It is the civilization of this era that, having weighed, he finds wanting—not in the spirit of Rousseau, idealizing the "natural man," but because this civilization "is immoral, impoverishing, and turning man away from himself, making an object out of him."[4] Many of his Western contemporaries held similar opinions; but among Polish writers of the post-Romantic period, Norwid stood alone with his determined and not emotionally but morally and philisophically based opposition forcefully expressed in *Civilization*.

III *The Italian Trilogy*

The correspondence of Norwid's last years shows what frantic efforts he was making to break away from the melancholy state of affairs which had forced him to move into the St. Casimir Asylum, how desperately he tried to get away—if only for a few months—from this home for Polish veterans on the outskirts of Paris. He wanted to go to Italy or to the South of France to cure his lung condition, but such a trip required money. His three novelettes sometimes called the "Italian trilogy" were born out of his desire to raise enough money to enable him to escape. Years of bitter experience had taught Norwid that poetry did not sell. He hoped that stories, published in a pamphlet form, would do the trick. The "Italian trilogy" written in 1882 and 1883 represents Norwid's most mature achievement in narrative prose, although, as had happened with so many other manuscripts, Norwid did not live to see its publication.

Yet even these novelettes are unusual for the age in which they were written, the age of Maupassant and Henry James. All three are more stories of "setting" than of action. They have slight and "intentionally inadequate" plots [5] in which the author concentrates on one event of special significance; this event and its consequences are commented upon in a philosophical (*Stigma*) or ironical (*Ad Leones, Lord Singleworth's Secret*) manner. Consequently, they show little similarity with either the naturalistic or the realistic kind of short story. Although they have more narrative than Norwid's "legends" and are more coherent in their structure than his "flowers," these novelettes are in fact moralistic tales conceived in the spirit of socially critical symbolism. In other words, even when trying to work "for the market" Norwid was unable to conform to the taste and requirements of the market: pure entertainment, a good story for its own sake, was anathema to him.

In *Stigma* (*Stygmat*), the first and longest of the three stories, Norwid elaborates a truth familiar to students of heredity and psychology; namely, each person is determined to some extent by his origins, family circumstances, and upbringing, in a word, by his past. It is the "stigmas" of the past that wreck the love affair of the talented Oscar and the strikingly beautiful Rosalie. Their love unfolds before the narrator who at that time lives at a small Italian spa, but the relationship is fatally disturbed and breaks up through a misunderstanding. Oscar misinterprets the tone of Rosalie's voice on a certain occasion. Oscar is a violinist, a young widower, whose neurotic sensitivity makes him overreact to harsh tones. The unfortunate Rosalie, on the other hand, while nursing her deaf father had acquired a tone of speaking louder than usual. These individual peculiarities are the stigmas which lead to alienation. The end of the affair is tragic: Rosalie contracts pneumonia, as a result of Oscar's behavior, and dies, while Oscar retires to a monastery. It is not clear, however, why Norwid did not end his novelette at this point instead of continuing it with the sketch of a romantic essay. The essay stylized as a dream is a historiosophic extension of the theory of stigmas, applicable to individuals, nations, and historical personalities. Both parts, interesting in themselves, have little relevance to each other. Moreover, the dream is followed by two further episodes—one realistic, the other perhaps symbolic—neither of which adds much to the understanding of the whole story or to our comprehension of Norwid's theory of stigmas.

In *Lord Singleworth's Secret* (*Tajemnica Lorda Singlewortha*) the hero, an eccentric English lord, attracts much attention in Venice with his periodic excursions into higher regions carried out with the aid of a balloon. Here the symbol is almost self-explanatory, but Norwid is didactic enough to have his lordship himself answering inquiries as to the cause of his escapades. He cannot stand the "low" baseness, the uncleanliness of the "civilized world," the towns of which are built and flourish over "cesspools," the elegant salons of which are not very far from "heavy and frightening underground vaults." Lord Singleworth sees clearly the social price of society's "cleanliness" which degrades and reduces to an "unclean" status countless people employed to clean away society's dirt. At the end of his speech about cleanliness, Lord Singleworth declares: "People are not yet clean—they are only perfumed. . . ." [6] Soon afterwards he takes off in his balloon, in other words he opts out of society. In the absence of any realistic program to reform society, this very aristocratic form of protest is approved by Norwid. He, too, considers the epoch morally unclean (anything that degrades a human being is "unclean"), and Lord Singleworth's balloon expresses the symbolic rejection of the morally polluted world in which he lives.

The critical accents are even stronger in *Ad leones*, the third story of the "Italian trilogy." This brief but remarkable story gives the quintessence of Norwid's views on the debasement of art in a mercantile society. The style is more vivid and vigorous than in any of the other stories, the irony more explicit, yet at the same time more complex than in *Lord Singleworth's Secret*. Norwid sets his story in Rome, where in his youth he used to frequent the Café Greco, a meetingplace of artists and art critics. His red-bearded sculptor-hero is rumored to be working on a composition provisionally called *Ad leones!* representing the martyrdom of

two Christians thrown to the lions at the time of the Emperor
Domitian. The sculptor invites some friends and potential cus-
tomers to his studio to view the work in progress. During the
visit certain changes suggested by the group are carried out. First,
the cross is eliminated from the Christians' hands. Then it is suggested that after all the figures need not be Christian martyrs
at all, "they may in fact represent struggle, sacrifice, or in fact
merit." [7] Finally, an American correspondent enters the scene and
after suggesting some minor changes buys the composition which
for him represents Capitalism, the apotheosis of thrift, energy,
and work. What Norwid shows here can be equally deplored
from a personalist Christian or a Marxist point of view: how the
work of art, originally expressing the artist's vision, turns into a
marketable commodity; how, with the active cooperation of the
opportunistic artist, his sculpture becomes a product of alienation,
the very opposite of his original intentions.

The question as to who is the main target of Norwid's irony and
criticism in *Ad leones* has been much discussed in critical literature. Yet in a sense, this question is almost irrelevant. True, the
editor of a political and literary gazette and the tutor of a young
tourist suggest the crucial changes, and the rich American correspondent completes the debasement of the original idea by placing
his order for "Capitalism," yet the sculptor is equally responsible
for the final outcome of his work, since he accepts the changes
without a murmur. Whereas at the beginning of the story it is
easy to subscribe to the opinion of the "thoughtful observer" who
gains a favorable impression of the sculptor's "spiritual dignity,"
in the end we are convinced that he is less a serious artist than a
skillful craftsman. True, he finds himself in a vicious circle. In
art, as in everything, the market dictates taste and popularity, and
the artist needs unusual self-discipline and determination to refuse the demands of "society," in this case the moneyed bourgeois.
"Redaction is reduction," the editor laconically observes, but in
Norwid's eyes this reduction spells treason. The price of success
is the betrayal of one's own principles, the "reduction" of art's
richness and complexities to the vulgar taste of the esthetically
illiterate consumer. The idea of real art is thrown to the lions—
hence the title *Ad leones* is doubly appropriate and is full of
irony. *Ad leones* is one of the few prose works in which Norwid
successfully blended his esthetic views and his social criticism

with his chosen art form. This story is equal, if not superior, to the best poems of Norwid's last poetic period.

Nevertheless, Norwid was above all a poet, and this is reflected in the quality of his prose as well as in his attitude toward the novel which was, on the whole, scornful and hostile. Writing to Kraszewski, a prolific novelist and a Jack-of-all-trades in Polish literature, he confessed that he had not read more than three novels in his whole life.[8] Whether this was due to his "arbitrary position of superiority" and desire to be a nonconformist in yet another way is debatable.[9] In his letter to Kraszewski, written in 1858, Norwid uses the word *romans* rather than the proper Polish word for a novel, *powieść*. This indicates that at least part of Norwid's aversion to this genre was connected with his dislike for the new and rapidly growing fashion of the *roman-feuilleton*, or serial novel printed in newspapers. In his eyes the French novel was represented more by Eugène Sue, George Sand, and the elder Dumas, than by Stendhal and Flaubert. (Stendhal, whose *The History of Italian Painting* Norwid read with appreciation, became popular only in the 1880's.) As for the Polish novel, before Bolesław Prus and Henryk Sienkiewicz it existed at best on a prerealist, that is, fairly primitive, level. Though the Polish romantics read Walter Scott, his influence did not lead them to the historical novel. Instead they wrote poetic tales or "novels" in verse. The social novel had been considered a "low" genre by most educated people in Norwid's youth. Though he could read French and Italian, and later on English, tolerably well, Norwid thought it a waste of time to read popular French novels when he could read Dante, Shakespeare, Byron, and Victor Hugo. A deeper reason for Norwid's lack of interest in the novel could be found in his overall view of the epoch. He felt that the novel, preoccupied as it was with social conflicts, would mainly describe the life of the industrial, materialistic, bourgeois society which he detested with all his heart. He suspected that just as the age was ahistorical in essence, so too, the novel, the mirror image of this society, was just skirting the edge of the real, that is, universally relevant, problems. Until Tolstoy this view could to some extent be justified, and as far as we know Norwid never heard of *War and Peace*. At any rate, he was not a born storyteller, nor was he interested in the particularities of the world; he wanted to grasp its totality through the poetic identification of the truth shaping mankind's destiny.

IV *The Słowacki Lectures*

Apart from short stories and prose parables Norwid wrote many articles and short essays on such diverse subjects as the fine arts, music, archaeology, the tasks of the Polish press, women's emancipation, the philosophy of political action, and, finally, Polish literature. Though some of his writings on art, namely, the essay *About Art: For Poles* (*O sztuce dla Polaków*), would be of interest not only to art historians but also to students of Norwid's thought, the texts which are most central to Norwid's life and *oeuvre* are two literary and historiosophic essays: the Słowacki lectures and *Silence*.

The six public lectures on Juliusz Słowacki and the appendix on Słowacki's *Balladyna*, later added to the text, were published together in booklet form soon after Norwid gave them. The lectures were delivered, probably from notes, in the Polish Reading Room in Paris from April to May, 1860. They were noted down by several members of the audience who then brought the text to Norwid for authorization. The Słowacki lectures are full of important hints and statements shedding light on Norwid's poetics and *Weltanschauung*. He discusses not only Słowacki but the tasks of poetry in general and refers to the situation of the poet in the post-Romantic period.

In the first lecture Norwid attempts to define the role which poets have been playing in society since the beginnings of literacy. After the poet-prophets of the Jews, the poet-priests and poet-heroes of the Greeks, poets suffered a certain loss of their high social status and in Rome they were "professionalized," becoming "mere poets." After Christ the mission of poets changed, since they were needed by their communities to serve the new national languages. Their task was to raise the language of the people to a high literary level. The poet of the present epoch, says Norwid, is facing a double task. On the one hand, he has to "unravel the speech of centuries in the mouth of the Sphinx," while on the other, he should create anew "Christian speech" whenever it is drifting toward "the idolatry of form alone" and through that back to a kind of heathen cult.[10] In other words, the real poet must have an awareness of the past and a desire to mold his own epoch, correcting the march of mankind toward the future whenever it is deflected from its course.

Since the poet's duties are defined within the framework of Christianity, or rather within Christian civilization, it is not surprising that Norwid formulates the poet's main task in a way strikingly similar to that of the apostles. He must bear witness to truth both in words and in deeds. This is why Norwid pays the highest tribute to Lord Byron, stating at the end of his first lecture: "Byron is—*the Socrates of poets*, for he managed to bring the poetic element into life and realize it in action, knowing what he was doing . . . *Ecce poeta!*"[11]

Significantly, in his second lecture Norwid continues to discuss the state of Christian civilization and Byron's true stature in the same breath. Christ's sacrifice and "victory" did not solve mankind's problems. It did not free each individual from the task of self-perfection and from his duties toward others. In fact, Christian civilization is permeated by "elements of barbarity" and heathenism. It remains for the man of the nineteenth century "to humanize philosophy, to make politics and economics Christian in spirit," which has not been done throughout nineteen centuries. On this criticism Norwid builds his myth of a Lord Byron resplendent with Christian virtues. He refuses to accept the widely held view that the essence of Byronism is disillusionment, eloquent skepticism, or elegant cynicism; on the contrary, he asserts that "Byron was more religious than his Church and his age. . . ."[12] He stood for the emancipation of Catholics in England. While his birth assured him high social standing, he took the side of the poor and the exploited. Here Norwid quotes Byron's letter to Lord Holland written just before his maiden speech in the House of Lords: ". . . we must not allow mankind to be sacrificed to improvements in mechanism."[13] In another passage, Norwid praises the English poet's courage and self-sacrificing support of the Greek cause. This episode in Byron's life, sealed by his death, makes him in Norwid's eyes the only great "cosmopolitan" hero of the past century, greater than Napoleon himself, comparable only to Kościuszko. He grows into the symbol of a whole epoch embodying the Romantic struggle for freedom. It is an epoch started at Missolonghi, but "Louis Kossuth is ending it before our eyes." While not hiding his emotional attachment to it, Norwid is aware of the fact that the

Romantic period has come to an end. This means new tasks, new perspectives, and a different kind of poetry.

Słowacki was, of course, a Romantic, and Norwid is convinced that he was one of the finest Romantic poets. From his lectures it looks as if he had most regard for three particular works by Słowacki: *Anhelli, Beniowski,* and *King Spirit (Król-Duch)*. The analysis of *Anhelli* is preceded by a protracted discourse on civilization. In Norwid's opinion all civilizations are relative, being only the means of mankind's self-realization, and should be regarded as scaffoldings for a building in construction. Christian civilization should not be idealized or idolized either; one of its gravest deficiencies is its inability to create socal justice. Civilizations are organic; they are born and they die; they also have a "positive" and a "negative" pole. For the United States, says Norwid, the negative pole is the question of American Negro rights, for England—Ireland; for Russia—Poland. For Poland, Siberia is "the point of twilight of her civilization," and it is here that we come to *Anhelli,* Słowacki's prose poem taking place in Siberia. Discussing Słowacki's "masterpiece," Norwid defines Anhelli, the much-suffering hero of the poem, as "the personification of the human heart in relation to the tragedy of history." [14] The symbolism in *Anhelli* is both universal and Polish; Norwid specially admires it for its "prophetic" character which is quite different from Mickiewicz's prophecies in *The Books of the Polish Nation and Pilgrimage (Księgi narodu i pielgrzymstwa polskiego)*. The anti-Mickiewicz core of his praise for Słowacki is clearly revealed in a barb dismissing "Wallenrodism" as "a romantic tale" and putting forward "Winkelriedism" as a countercredo to the cult of romantic revenge.[15] These two names, originating in Mickiewicz's and Słowacki's works respectively, were symbols of alternate ways of struggle against Poland's enemies: "Wallenrodism" standing for the Machiavellian and ruthless, "Winkelriedism" for the self-sacrificing and ethical approach. In view of his moral and political convictions, Norwid's choice is not at all surprising.

Norwid, in a sense, tried to define his own position through Słowacki. A case in point is the question of obscurity, an accusation sometimes raised against Słowacki, especially against his works from "the mystical period." In connection with *King Spirit,* which is undoubtedly one of Słowacki's most difficult and obscure works, Norwid raises the question whether everything that is great must be entirely clear. His answer is "no," since there are unclear parts in Mickiewicz and Krasiński, Dante and Shakespeare as well. Life itself is unclear; it is full of "dramatic aspects" and complexities which cannot be presented without a certain element of opacity. True, mirrors are clear, but they are also flat and art is not simply reflection. Elaborating this argument Norwid censures Science, or rather the almost religious worship of science so characteristic of his age: "The so-called exact sciences . . . draw the clarity of their theories from the fact that their goal is only *half of the truth*, hence I would rather call them *inexact* in relation to truth."[16]

As for Juliusz Słowacki, Norwid assigns him a place of honor in the pantheon of Polish poetry. In this respect also he was a precursor of later developments, as only the generation of Young Poland (*Młoda Polska*) recognized Słowacki's true stature. In his last lecture Norwid praised Słowacki's unparalleled mastery of the language, for the author of *Beniowski* could speak the language of all epochs, societies, human types, and sexes. In the great division of labor among the three "bards" (*wieszcze*) of Polish Romanticism, Słowacki's task was the perfection of the language.

Norwid thought highly of Słowacki's plays as well; this is more than obvious from the appendix to the Słowacki lectures devoted entirely to *Balladyna* of which Norwid gave an interesting, though to some extent overly symbolic, interpretation. While he admired *Balladyna*, Norwid shared the feeling of most contemporaries that Słowacki's play was too "figurative," altogether too poetic to be staged successfully. He had no such fears about *Lilla Weneda*, *Salome's Silver Dream*, and *Mazepa*; he did not hesitate to place them above the works of the best-known playwrights of the Warsaw theater.[17]

In his lectures on Słowacki, Norwid revealed a critical ability, not practiced by him very often either in émigré or in the Poznań or Cracow newspapers. The reasons for this were probably mixed. Reviews were badly paid, if paid at all; he did not have the time, and, more important, he did not have the energy to quarrel with editors who failed to print and lost his poems, or wrote sarcastic notes on his "hieroglyphs" and "phantasies." He could not work for the literary market, and the literary establishment, insofar as it existed in the various partitions and in Paris, viewed him with suspicion, if not outright hostility. That is why apart from the Słowacki lectures most of Norwid's literary criticism remained private in his lifetime—buried in letters and notes published only many years later.

V Silence

Silence (*Milczenie*), a long essay written a year before his death, is Norwid's last comprehensive attempt to expound his views on poetics and on the dialectics of history. As a piece of prose *Silence* appears to be less coherent than some of Norwid's earlier prose writings. The contemporary reader finds it too verbose and parts of it marred by a somewhat pedantic exposition of Greek philosophy and certain, perhaps unnecessary, digressions. Nevertheless, in this essay Norwid makes some theoretical points of great interest. First of all, he presents *przemilczenie* (incomplete statement) as an important feature of speech which is on the whole completely ignored by grammarians. We have translated *przemilczenie* here as "incomplete statement," having referred to it earlier as "unsaying" or "leaving things unsaid." It cannot be fully translated into English, for apart from the negative aspects indicated above, it actually involves (at least in its Norwidian sense) also the implication of something positive but hidden for the time being. Thus the statement or sentence A is understood to contain *przemilczenie* A [1], and this A [1], the unstated part in sentence A, has a central function in the next sentence, B. In fact, it *becomes* the essential statement of sentence B which, however, leaves something else, i.e., B [1], unstated as well; thus a chain is formed. This "linguistic" recognition becomes the core of Norwid's view on history: ". . . what had been the *przemilczenie* of the intellectual totality of one Epoch, becomes the "message" (*wygłos*) of the literature of a second Epoch in the following century." [18] His contention is followed by examples, the first being the case of the Orphic hymn singing Zeus' omnipotence. This text, written in the Epoch of the Legend, involves at least one significant omission: it leaves out man. So the next epoch, under the sign of the Epos, starts with the poet praising the exploits of a human individual, Odysseus. For Norwid only Homer "completes" the Orphic hymns.

As we have seen, the author of *Silence* proposes a dialectical method of his own, a non-Hegelian kind of historic and intellectual evolution. Each epoch keeps silent on one issue or another, but the chances are that if the issue in question is important, it will be revealed in the next epoch. As for his division of history into epochs, Norwid's conception is thoroughly Romantic. The first is the Epoch of the Legend, followed by that of the Epos, and then the Epoch of History. The fourth epoch, roughly coinciding with the nineteenth century, is the Epoch of the Anecdote. This is a profoundly "ahistorical" age which produces only "novels and tales" in literature. It is interesting to compare Norwid's views with the strictures of the Marxist philosopher and critic Georg Lukács on the post-1849 period: "History as a total process disappears; in its place there remains a chaos to be ordered as one likes"; and somewhat later "history becomes a collection of exotic anecdotes." [19] The Epoch of the Anecdote, however, is to be followed by the Epoch of the Revolution—by "our great Christian Revolution" which is identical with the Revelation. What Norwid had in mind here was certainly different from the revolutionary movements of the nineteenth century; what he meant was a revolutionary change in human morals and attitudes, bringing about the realization of Christian ideals in the life of nations and communities. Though the social criticism is similar to that of the Marxists', the vision of the future evokes Cieszkowski.

Both Norwid's style and intellectual categories in this essay are more poetic than scholarly. But even if we dismiss his classification of history into five epochs as irrelevant to the real development of history, the theory of *przemilczenie* has interesting philosophical and esthetic implications. Social and historical progress appears, for instance, in less rigid schemata than the inexorable clash of the "thesis" with the "antithesis" ending in the triumph of the "synthesis." Norwid does not envisage a real synthesis, but implies that evolution is a self-correcting process, each new thesis being in some ways antithetical to the previous one and through its incompleteness also antithetical to the next one. Though he is an evolutionist, he does not believe in random selection or "the survival of the fittest" but in a mysterious process of selection, and accepts not only the survival but the eventual triumph of an artist's *personal truth*, misunderstood or incompletely understood in his lifetime.

VI *Norwid in His Letters*

Not too prolific as a writer of fiction and rarely venturing into the field of literary criticism, Norwid kept up a lifelong engagement in one particular kind of prose: in letter-writing. While among his contemporaries Słowacki's letters to his mother provide a useful background to his life and art, and Krasiński's letters to Delfina Potocka illuminate the exalted heights and self-tormenting abyss of Romantic love, Norwid's letters are addressed to a variety of persons and run the whole gamut of emotions and thought. These letters shed light on Norwid's simple and frugal way of life, his difficult living circumstances, his fight to survive as a painter and a poet against overwhelming odds. At the same time they serve as a vehicle for his ideas, esthetic, social, and political views, and opinions on his more or less distinguished contemporaries. Over a thousand of Norwid's letters survived, out of which Przesmycki published more than eight hundred in the 1930's. Since then some important new finds have been made, the results of which have been published by Stefania Skwarczyńska, Stanisław Pigoń, and others; even as late as 1970 some previously unknown letters of Norwid's came to light.

Some of these letters are crucial for the understanding of a poem or a play, others are simply variations on themes discussed elsewhere in poems or in newspaper articles. The tone of his letters conveys Norwid's suffering in an alien environment, his encounters with few friends but with many casual acquaintances, his mental agonies over the fate of Poland and the desperate state of Polish society. In the case of the latter Norwid often deplored its ignorance of truth, its lack of appreciation of real literature, and its indifference or hostility toward the most outstanding individuals in its recent history. Since the letters, with few exceptions, were written for private use, Norwid's tone is much more bitter and sarcastic, his outbursts more frequent and less controlled, than in other writings. Apart from letters requesting or giving factual information, by and large there are two, though often intermingling, kinds of letters: "didactic" and "emphatic" ones. For one reason or another most "didactic" letters were written to women (Maria Trębicka, Joanna Kuczyńska, Konstancja Górska), while the "emphatic" ones were written to men who more often than not belonged to Norwid's own generation. This is understandable; if one complains, it is preferable to complain to people of a similar background, age, and experience. In the first kind of letter there is more discussion of philosophy and esthetics, while in the second emotional generalizations and axiomatic statements based on Norwid's personal experience predominate. As previously stated, however, there is no rigid line of division between these two types. One of Norwid's best known and most frequently quoted letters (written to August Cieszkowski in November, 1850), for instance, contains a short exposition of Norwid's philosophical views or general outlook, but it is also a passionate confession of his own homelessness and alienation from society. There are others of the "emphatic" type in which in two or three short paragraphs a whole drama unfolds. A letter written to General Mierosławski during the siege of Paris in 1870 is worth quoting in full:

Dear General!

I was just walking somewhere—deaf, ill, sad and deep in thought, with a copy-book and pencil in my hand, when someone exclaimed: "*Espion prussien.*" I have been wading through the foam of this incredible affair suffering pangs of irony. Do kindly send a letter to someone of importance at present and do it properly; I know that you can do that. Let them know who I am. Because with my disability (*z kalectwem moim*) which I acquired in a damp Prussian jail in 1846 and with pain on my face, if someone dislikes the shape of my nose again I shall have more trouble, and as you can see, I have trouble enough.

Some person, unknown to me, but wearing a *czamarka*, flung himself there when they were leading me away and protested—I laughed and cried in my heart. One person at least!

C.N.[20]

Norwid's epistolary style is a mixture of long, carefully composed and short, nervous sentences. Neologisms are as frequent here as in his prose or poems: they are clearly not mannerisms but the results of Norwid's creative imagination which often resorted to improvisation in its effort to find the most adequate expression. As in other writings, Norwid's idiosyncratic typography asserts itself in his letters as well. He underlines or capitalizes whole phrases even more often than elsewhere. Occasionally, he switches into French, or uses French expressions in Polish letters (though a certain amount of his correspondence was entirely in French, with people like Herzen or Emma Herwegh). In general, Norwid's style does not please purists. His newly coined words are often adaptations from the French (and they are not always successful), a development understandable if ones takes into account the length of his separation from Poland and his ambition to keep abreast, both intellectually and verbally, with new phenomena in the arts and in science. One could say that the style of Norwid's letters is eclectic in a manner which nevertheless conveys the extraordinary integrity of his character and also the dignity and imaginative force of his language, archaic and modern at the same time.

As so many of the letters, the last one (March, 1883) is a cry for help, for help which is not forthcoming. The whole tragedy of an artist's life in exile, of a great *oeuvre* not appreciated by contemporaries, is contained in these melancholy lines: "C. N. deserved two things from Polish Society: that this society should not be *alien* and *hostile* towards him." [21]

CHAPTER 7

Against Slavery

I Christian Universalism

AFTER the discussion of Norwid's achievement in various literary genres, it is now appropriate to assess, at least in general outlines, his *Weltanschauung* and philosophy of life. What is particularly interesting is the unity of his thought and its reflection in his creative work. Consequently, the chronological approach applied in previous chapters has to be abandoned, and Norwid's thought will be evaluated from a thematic and structural point of view.

Norwid's philosophy is based on a deep awareness of the human predicament seen through the prism of Christian faith and on a conscious engagement for real progress, a desire to participate in the process of history. His outlook is Christian, dialectical, historicist, and anthropocentric; his intellect and language are constantly groping for a synthesis capable of transcending the limitations of both traditional Catholic philosophy (whether in its Thomist or later versions) as well as German idealism. All the same, Norwid did not erect a coherent philosophical system of his own. Such a system exists in his writings only in bare outline, and it is generally camouflaged by poetic language and elliptic turns of speech. As a poet he was certainly "philosophizing" but without the ambition of becoming a philosopher.

Nevertheless, certain basic ideas consistently emerge from Norwid's poems and prose writings. An important source, almost an inventory, of his historiosophic thought is the *Epilogue* to the poetic treatise *Slavery* (*Niewola*). "I believe that the goal is *the perfection of all*/To be *realized* gradually—for the whole." [1] In other words, Norwid shared the views of Hoene-Wroński, Ballanche, Cieszkowski, and other antimaterialistic philosophers of the nineteenth century that the history of mankind was but a search for the road leading back to the Absolute, that though he had fallen from grace, man is perfectible, since his higher destiny is to attain perfection. Such an evolution, however, was not possible without a harmony of historical (social and national) and individual human progress. Negation or neglect of either of these factors leads to serious setbacks, delays, and distortions, to Vico's *ricorsi*. In Norwid's view the individual can develop his qualities through creative work and brotherly love, while historical progress can be furthered through acts of sacrifice, especially of a "Christian" kind. This idea originated with Ballanche, in the center of whose philosophy stands the idea of work as expiation. The division between work and sacrifice is not rigid and is often blurred; which of the two is called for at a given point in history depends on historical circumstances. Socrates and Saint Paul, Copernicus and Kościuszko can coexist in Norwid's pantheon; each is a hero in his own right. The poet, as well as the philosopher, has to be able to read "the book of history"; he can understand the present only through the past and can develop an action program only through interpreting the actual moment in history. God is present in history but only through man.

In other words, Norwid believes in mankind's progress through history and in its eventual "rebirth" in the sign of the Holy Spirit. His thought, however, just like Cieszkowski's, is dialectical and flexible enough to make allowances for eventual setbacks and deformations which from time to time cast a shadow on his long-term historiosophic optimism. Social development favors institutionalization, or in Norwid's terminology "formalization," form taking precedence over content: "*Slavery—is the substitution / Of the aim by form. That is oppression. . . .*" [2] If the nation can be compared to a living organism, and according to Norwid it certainly can, then any form of government that is alien from its subject, the nation, is either a cancerous growth or an empty husk containing no spirit. From this it follows that the greatest political sin is the absolutism of any political idea, whether it be "conservatism" (which Norwid approves only in its "enlightened" form), "democracy," or "socialism." Such an act will lead to tyranny in one form or another.

Toward the end of Song I in *Slavery*, Jesus is invoked as a prophet who did not break the Law but filled it with the radiant light of freedom; who, though he came armed only with an olive branch, managed to subdue the greatest of all empires. *"Let us not be human slaves"* Norwid goes on, *"For there's freedom where God's spirit keeps vigil."* [3] "Human slaves" here has the connotation of "mankind's slaves." As for the second half of Norwid's message comprised in these lines, it shows clearly the Christian character of his ontology. Christian is a more appropriate word here than Catholic, although Norwid certainly considered himself a loyal and faithful Catholic. All the same, his Christianity asserted itself in a "universalistic approach" which "in the times when he lived was nearly close to heresy." [4] The Church which Norwid postulated and approved in his heart included everyone whose actions rather than nominal religious allegiance were Christian. Only on such premises can we understand his openly expressed admiration for self-sacrificing or noble individuals belonging to other than Catholic denominations (John Brown, Abd-el-Kader), for people whose behavior was generally considered non-Christian by contemporaries (Byron), or even for renegades (General Bem who embraced Islam in order to join the Turkish Army). As for the official Roman Catholic Church Norwid's attitude toward it was loyal but not uncritical. It was mainly his strong distaste for the unseemly political maneuvering and tactical compromises of this Church that made him confess to Cieszkowski in 1850: "In relation to the *Church* —which I have had the idea of entering and I have worked on it within myself—I say this: should I become a monk today, *I would commit heresy tomorrow.*" [5] Nevertheless, four years later, during the last months of his stay in New York, when he had sunk into a state of melancholic depression "bordering on madness," he would write desperate letters to his former confessor in Paris, asking his permission to join the Order of the Resurrectionists. The confessor's answer was negative, and he was probably right from the Order's point of view. While Norwid's way of life was ascetic enough to put a monk to shame, his social and political views (still in a state of ferment for over another decade) might easily have led him—if not into "heresy," then to serious conflicts with his superiors. Among leading French Catholic politicians he had a special respect for Montalambert, whom he knew personally,[6] and whose "reformist" Catholicism had surely appealed to him. Nevertheless, in a private letter he expressed his complete

approval for the papal encyclical *Quanta Cura* which is generally
described by historians as a reactionary and anti-Montalambertist
document. Perhaps what most influenced his judgment in this
case was Pius IX's sympathy for the Polish cause, clearly demon-
strated by the Pope during the 1863–64 uprising.[7]
Norwid's universalist Christianity is closely connected with his
appraisal of Christ's significance. He is called in *Slavery* "a real
God and a real man"; he is the ideal to be followed rather than
imitated.[8] This is an important distinction, for it shows Norwid's
belief in the autonomy of the human personality and his affinity
with an "apostolic" rather than a "mystical" model of Christian
initiation. Apart from the divine principle he embodied, Christ
gave an entirely new meaning to the word "man." This is where
Norwid's Christianity links up with his anthropocentrism. Now-
where else in nineteenth-century Polish poetry has "man" such
dignity as in Norwid's writings; nowhere else has he the same
profound and complex quality. On the one hand, Norwid's man is
"an ignorant and immature priest"[9] who has not yet grasped his
destiny, on the other hand, he is "God's neighbor," potentially
perfectible, capable of reaching the highest level in human evolution, that of "God-Man." The dialectics of this duality sometimes depress Norwid, while at other times prompt him to such
statements, impressive in their stoic dignity, as the following:

> . . . laurel and hope may be the share of others,
> I—have only one honor: that I am a man.[10]

II *We Are One Huge National Flag*

His apostolic Christianity and consistent anthropocentrism
made Norwid antagonistic to certain schools of idealistic philosophy. Although attempts have been made to link Norwid's
thought with that of Hegel,[11] the closest one gets in tracing these
connections and influences is August Cieszkowski, whose critique
of Hegel was such an important step in the political development
of the post-Hegelian Left. Cieszkowski started out as a Hegelian,
but by the time he published his magnum opus *Our Father*
(*Ojcze-Nasz*), he had moved far away from his erstwhile master.
Norwid thought highly of Cieszkowski and carried on an ani-
mated correspondence with this modern "Socrates." Thus Hegelian
influences, if at all, reached him through Cieszkowski's critical

sieve. Moreover, especially in the early 1850's, Norwid repeatedly made scathing remarks on "German philosophy" or "German ideology" for its historical determinism and aprioristic abstractness. His condemnation of "German philosophy" (which is not unlike the criticism made by Libelt and other representatives of what was broadly called the school of "Polish national philosophy"), though conveyed in general terms, indicates a definite aversion to any system based on "the tyranny of reason." There are other passages in Norwid's writings that are anti-Hegelian in their import. The author of *Promethidion* contrasts the nation with the state in a way which makes the latter appear as an epitome of slavery. In a philosophy-saturated letter written to the Poznań-based *Polish Daily* (*Dziennik Polski*) in 1849, Norwid defined the nation as "the internal alliance of related races" and followed this up with the distinction: "so the *nation* arises from the spirit, consequently from will and freedom . . . but the *state* is [formed] from the body, or rather it comes *from outside, from this* world—from unfreedom." [12] Anyone who tried to work for "God's Kingdom" by-passing the nation, which Norwid equated with "God's spirit in man and man in history," was obviously doing the wrong thing. Here and in other articles not only the state but by implication all forms fo racism and class-Messianism were condemned. One can work for mankind only through one's nation. For while the Church is "beyond History" and the race or the tribe is "below History," only the nation is really in the mainstream of History.[13] To ignore or to deny national rights in the name of a state, an abstract "mankind," or "universal brotherhood" is in Norwid's words "to rape time."

Would the views described above qualify Norwid as a Polish nationalist? Not at all. To realize the importance of the nation as an "organic" and unavoidable entity does not necessarily make one the adherent of a nationalistic, that is, by definition an exclusive and ethnocentric, ideology. Norwid stressed often that what he called "national" should not be interpreted as "exclusive," adding *"the nation consists not only of the spirit which differs from others but also of that which links it [to others]."*[14] While remaining throughout his life a patriot who passionately believed in Poland's right to independence and in the reemergence of a free Poland in the rather distant future, his conviction did not influence his views on the historical role and limitations of the

nation. The following taken from a letter dating from 1852 can
be regarded as the quintessence of Norwid's attitude to this question: "A nation has an existence to the extent that it is capable of
respecting the human individual." [15] It was not lack of respect
for authority or for royal power that destroyed independent
Poland but its *"disregard for man as a person"* (*nieuszanowanie
osoby-człowieka*).[16] In other words the privileged classes of the
old republic (*Rzeczpospolita*) did not practice the Christian virtues they had professed in words. There can be no doubt that in
the quotation above Norwid speaks not as a sage of the Enlightenment but as a consistent Christian. There are interesting similarities between his views on nationalism and those of some modern
religious thinkers, notably Berdayev.[17]

Norwid viewed Poland's strongest enemy, Russia, from a patriotic and Christian universalist standpoint. Unlike Mickiewicz
he had little personal contact with Russians (apart from Alexander Herzen and Ivan Turgenev, neither of whom he knew
well, and at the end of his life Piotr Lavrov) and categorically
rejected Pan-Slavism as early as 1848. Moreover, in the early
1840's he and his contemporaries experienced Russian oppression
in a more brutal form than many older émigrés and consequently
had no illusions about the possibility of a miraculous understanding between the two nations. By and large one can recognize the
existence of "two Russias" in Norwid's thought: the first one, to
some extent a "mythologized," totally negative and repulsive
Russia, usually taking precedence over the second one, the socially differentiated and internally changing and developing country.[18] What strikes Norwid in the Russian state is its "inorganic"
and culturally alien, epigonistic character: "Russia . . . is not a
nation but a *formal state.*" [19] In another letter, while describing
Russia as a "young and materially strong" nation, he writes with
a mixture of contempt and irony: "I am not surprised that the
Russian statesmen, almost all *atheists* with a slight and superficial philosophical veneer, imagine that *history* has only such
aspects as are manifested in congresses, in the strength of the
gendarmerie or in matters of finance." [20] His exasperation about—
as Tennyson put it—"the overgrown Barbarian in the East" flares
up again during the 1863 uprising and is vented in a poem entitled *To the Enemy*. Having scolded imperial Russia for its
slavish inertia and immobility, he flings into the face of the op-

pressor the most dramatic question of the Christian and freedom-loving martyr:

O! stop! pull back your bayonets—you—slave!
For how long shall I die *for you*? [21]

On the other hand, Norwid understood that Poland could ig-nore her geopolitical situation only at her own peril; that Russia was and would remain a neighbor "forever"; and that it is folly to give up the idea of influencing Russian public opinion. He wrote to Karol Ruprecht reflecting upon a criticism of American policy which, though upholding republican principles, main-tained friendly relations with despotic Russia:

Only free people, only persons who were not already in the cradle branded with hot iron as SLAVES are aware of the fact that if a country has a frontier with Russia it has to have there its OWN PARTY—for otherwise two monoliths will clash all the time . . . Mos-cow could have its party in Republican Poland . . . but the Poles in Russia have never attempted that—not having that much political sense! [22]

The argument that follows this statement is even more critical of Poles than of Russians. The Russians are what they are, but "the sin" of the Poles is that they never fight with their mind and in-tellect and have "no faith whatsoever in the power of thought and truth." They prefer armed insurrections instead and pay a regular blood-sacrifice to history, thus bleeding white each successive generation.

These last reflections actually introduce the next theme arising from the question of nationality—Norwid's complex relationship to his native country, society, and compatriots. While his set of ideas and opinions on these issues contain certain constant ele-ments (such as the condemnation of Sarmatism, a know-nothing chauvinistic orientation, or the glorification of great Poles of the past such as Sobieski and Kościuszko), in the second half of his life spent in exile both the volume and the bitterness of his criti-cism of specifically Polish vices kept growing. His denunciation of Polish sins and omissions became almost obsessive. One could fill a small anthology with Norwid's utterances on the subject, some of them perfectly justified, others understandable but rather exaggerated. Even the latter were the expression of frustrated love—it was in Polish that Norwid kept cursing and castigating his ignorant, vain, sluggish, and ungrateful countrymen. During his first years in Paris Norwid thought that he had begun to see what was missing from the mind of the typical Pole, a member of the *szlachta* (nobility) boasting more or less education. Such a person, he felt, though usually holding strong political views, was unable to understand either the moral of history or the mentality of most foreigners; he would be one-sided and unfair in his emotional nationalism and violent self-righteousness. This was particularly true of Norwid's own generation which grew up in a spirit of bitterness, eager for fighting and revenge. In a letter to Lenartowicz, Norwid condemned this mentality as blind, un-Christian, and despotic: "They love Poland like God and therefore they cannot bring her salvation, for what can you do for God?" [23] This, in Norwid's eyes, is idolatry. Some years later he came to a rather extreme conclusion which he again expressed in a terse, axiomatic statement: "We are not *a society* at all. We are one huge *national flag . . . Poland is the last society on earth and the first nation on the globe.*" [24] This paradox derived from Norwid's recognition of the lack of solidarity in Polish society, the lack of cohesiveness between various social groups, and from his conviction that few Poles have respect for the individual, unless he represents or embodies social or political power. The idea of the Polish nation is extolled by the Pole, but the reality of another human being who speaks the same language is ignored or despised. Norwid never tried to examine Polish society in systematic sociological terms but in the microcosm of the exile community certain things stood out with striking clearness. Most aristocrats gave little support to the Polish cause, let alone to Polish culture (Prince Czartoryski being an obvious exception); while the *szlachta*, on the whole of Democratic convictions, spent most of its time in eternal wrangling and brawls (hence Norwid's succinct definition of the Democrats camp: "it's like a Flemish tavern") and were on the whole indifferent to literature and the arts. However, Norwid's sarcasm is the most biting when he describes the situation of "*the intelligentsia*" inside partitioned Poland. "Nowhere on earth," he wrote in 1864, "is the Intelligentsia more dependent and more humiliated than in Poland. All persons who work intellectually are clients, poor dependent relatives (*rezydenty*), private tutors . . . without a permanent position." In another letter reflecting upon the same subject he added: "When the entire Intelligentsia consists of people without shoes or of lackeys, there can be no civil courage—and there is none either." [25] The Polish intelligentsia as a separate social group began to play a significant role for the first time during and after the 1863 uprising. What Norwid condemned in the letters quoted above was in fact the low status of the "intellectual workers," the Polish preintelligentsia, which had been tied to the landowning classes and to the whole feudal structure with many visible and invisible bonds. The fact, however, that "the intelligentsia," as such, hardly existed in Poland before 1864 was reflected in the attitudes of the aristocracy and the average nobleman *vis-à-vis* the Polish artist or intellectual living in emigration. Norwid could not expect recognition either for his work as an artist or for his status as an independent man of letters; this is perhaps why he brought up more than once in his correspondence the otherwise unimportant fact that he was on his mother's side related to the Sobieskis, a well-known aristocratic family.

Another recurring theme in Norwid's letters is Polish ingratitude and lack of appreciation for outstanding compatriots, sometimes amounting to insults and physical attacks on people who dared to infringe some national taboo. Norwid's list of such cases runs through practically the whole of Polish history starting with Piotr Skarga and ending with General Bem, Mierosławski, and the Polonophile English aristocrat Lord Dudley Stuart.[26] While he himself was not well-known and controversial enough to be physically attacked by political opponents, Norwid shared with most Polish poets and authors at least one form of humiliation: society's unwillingness to help in the publication of his manuscripts. The very fact that Norwid could not find a Polish publisher in his lifetime, with or without the help of a Krasiński or a Kraszewski (and not only in Paris but in Poland too), could be interpreted as proof of the immaturity and cultural backwardness of Polish society. As to the reading public, its bad taste and lack of sophistication were lamented in such characteristically Norwidian outbursts as: "*Always a mazurka!* Neither Poles nor the Polish language have an idea about real lyric poetry—what the

Poles call lyric verse is always a mazurka and the rhythm of peasant flails beating against the threshing floor. . . ." [27]

Most of these comments were not written for publication. In public statements and articles Norwid on the whole toned down the tenor of his criticism. He could not help feeling, however, that by exposing the weaknesses and shortcomings of the Polish character he was simply diagnosing an illness and thus helping to cure it. In this respect he took his cue from the much-admired Lord Byron who said many an unpleasant thing about his native land; and when accused of "fouling the nest," he retorted that those who stifled criticism were the real enemies of the healthy development of the national consciousness. [28] In spite of his passionate condemnation of certain typically Polish characteristics and numerous bitter remarks on the actual state of Polish society, Norwid needs no defense against the charge of anti-Polishness. When after the Crimean War the Tsar announced an amnesty for Polish émigrés Norwid asked the following, very relevant question:

> To which of the three am I allowed to return?
> To the *Fatherland?* to the *Country?* or to *Society?* [29]

He could have returned only to a Poland where the three were not separated from one another but formed an interdependent entity. It is clear from his correspondence that he did not feel at home even in that miniature Polish society that was functioning on the foundations laid down by the refugees of 1831. Where would he then feel at home? In the Polish language and in European history, his new "fatherland" being the historiosophic synthesis erected from wisdom and hope on the makeshift scaffolding of his idiosyncratic language.

III   *Ideas on Work*

We have already discussed the Norwidian idea of the poet's "mission" and the significance of the Word and of Faith in fighting the "unfreedom" of formalism, retrogression, and stagnation. These concepts would nevertheless remain rather elitist without their counterpart in the development of society—work. This aspect of Norwid's thought was touched on during the discussion of *Promethidion* but only in relation to art rather than to social philosophy.

Work and its role in the process of social evolution became a problem of the greatest consequence for Norwid in 1849, when on his arrival in Paris he found himself caught up in the slowly subsiding tremors of a strong social and political upheaval. Then, he first grasped the real motives behind the revolt of the masses and the swift rise of radical ideologies. He did this even to the point of understanding, though certainly not condoning, the atheism of such radicals as Proudhon ("every atheistic movement originates from the abuse of sacred things that had preceded it.")[30] In fact, Proudhon with his powerfully formulated anarchistic negation of the existing order continued to present a much stronger challenge to Norwid than did, for instance, the Positivists. It is conceivable that already *Four Pages of a Social Song* with its axiomatic reflections on property was meant as an indirect answer to Proudhon's famous dictum: "Property is theft." Many years later, soon after the Franco-Prussian war, Norwid found time to write an essay on Gustav Courbet which was mainly a refutation of Proudhon's crude esthetic views and misleading interpretation of Courbet's work. He did not waste much sympathy on Fourier either. What most alienated him philosophically from Mickiewicz was in fact the Fourier-like mystical radicalism of the great author of *The Forefathers' Eve*.[31] His generally critical attitude to what one could now call the "radical Leftist" theories of the period is clear from the short but incisive poem *Socialism*. It was the abstract, premature, and consequently "rapist" character of these theories that Norwid condemned, rather than the moral sentiment behind them. For in 1854 he made this memorable comment in a letter to Bohdan Zaleski: "Having wandered along the whole meridian of the civilized world from Naples to New York . . . I know, and not from the Socialists' theories, that destitution is endemic everywhere to such a practically ultimate degree that nobody pays enough attention to it." [32]

In other words Norwid was as much aware of the deficiencies and social injustice of the "civilized world" as any of his French, radical contemporaries, but he refused to accept the remedies offered by a Blanqui or a Proudhon. Already in *Promethidion* he connected the idea of work with creativity and understood that factories were indeed, as Michelet had claimed, "the real hell of ennui," because no worker was able to get satisfaction out of his monotonous and uninspiring work. In a free society, the character of work would also have to change. Drudgery excludes the possibility of freedom. And the other way around: "Where there is more freedom, there is also more work; and the freer the society, the more efficient is its work." [33] Norwid pointed to the contrast between the sad, sour, slavelike "forced work" that characterized backward societies such as for instance Persia or the Ukraine, the latter being part of historical Poland, and the freely sold labor of independent workingmen in the United States. (This can be read as praise of nonfeudal rather than capitalist labor.) "Work is originality," declared Norwid, condemning slavelike drudgery as a crossbreed between "the stock-exchange materialism of the West and the caste-bound materialism of the East." [34] The most interesting statement in this short essay entitled *To Spartacus: About Work* was, nevertheless, its final sentence: "Human work, although *it comes originally from expiation,* is not only not confined to the sorrows of expiation, but it certainly would be incomplete if it did not include the divine quality of Redemption (*Zbawstwo*)—in other words: it would be the aimless drudgery of helots!" [35] Mankind can make progress only through work and sacrifice: work that gives hope, and sacrifice that prepares the future.

Norwid's ideas on work are anti-Romantic inasmuch as he often contrasts the concept of creative work with that of the Romantic deed or gesture; but they cannot be called Positivistic either. This is borne out by, among other things, a close reading of the poem *Work (Praca)*, written in 1864. Here he scorns the school of those "realists" who advised the nation "to get rich as soon as possible"; in the poet's opinion the transition from "the bloody massacres of history to the workshops" cannot be made in one step.[36] Like the rising school of Warsaw Positivists Norwid also advocates "organic work," but he sees it in relation to the historical world-process, not only to the specific needs of contemporary Polish society. His thinking derives its arguments from his own intuition and artistic experience and is grounded in the categories of an exalted historiosophy. Organic work for him is not the peaceful continuation of the armed struggle, but the precondition of national self-therapy, the only serious alternative to a "recurrent massacre of innocents." Norwid also finds a new kind of heroism in work. In his poem *Hero (Bohater)*, after evoking previous models of heroism from Jason through Moses to the "spiritualized" hero of Christianity, he comes to the following conclusion:

> Let the age of the Colchians not return;
> I value the present equally well:
> *Heroism* will last as long as *work;*
> And work?—as long as creation! [37]

Mankind can be liberated only through creative work and well-timed sacrifices. Neither technology reducing people to robots nor "untimely" revolutions can further real liberation. Frustrated Christian, misunderstood patriot, and the forerunner of a "humanized," nonmaterialistic Socialism, Norwid believed in the future rebirth of mankind, knowing that the future would recognize in him an ally, a witness of a higher truth.

CHAPTER 8

Norwid's Reception—Past and Present

I Controversies with Contemporaries

THERE is hardly another poet or writer in the history of Polish letters who provoked so much hostility and rejection among critics as Cyprian Norwid. The widening gap between artist and public is a typical nineteenth-century phenomenon, but Norwid's case was different from those French Bohemians or esthetes who specialized in insulting the bourgeoisie while expecting to be supported by them. While we have referred earlier to hostile criticisms of certain aspects of Norwid's work, until now we have refrained from discussing the general causes of his conflict with the critics and, by implication, with the public contemporary to him.

Each artist is conditioned by the esthetic norms prevailing in his times. Such norms are often merely a codified form of the public's expectations. The poet of the Enlightenment was a rationalist who wrote in a didactic, moralistic or in a witty, elegant, and entertaining manner. He expected to be read by well-educated gentlemen who appreciated wisdom and enjoyed wit. The Romantic poet wrote for the middle-class individual. Rebelling against authority and convention, he asserted the rights of the heart and of imagination—qualities which had little to do with social rank or a classical education. Mickiewicz hoped that one day *Pan Tadeusz*, his epic poem, would find its way "under the thatched roofs" and be read by simple people, but in his lifetime it was read mostly by the Polish gentry who understood it as a glorification of their own past—a psychological factor which undoubtedly contributed to its popularity. Balzac's or Dickens's novels appealed to the middle-class reader with a keen interest in the details of everyday life and in the portrayal of people from his own social and economic milieu. While a great writer can present his vision of life to the general public, it is unlikely that he will find a responsive audience unless something in his work has a special appeal to a social class or group or at least to its most receptive members.

When Norwid chose poetry as the main vehicle for the expression of his emotions and ideas, though never giving up painting and sculpture as "subsidiary" forms of self-expression, he followed a tradition both Polish and Romantic. Poetry as conceived by him was not a kind of entertainment or the realization of his "unique individuality" but a moral duty to God and society: his duty to bear witness to truth. A moralistic trend is present in the work of most Polish poets revered by Norwid from Kochanowski through Krasicki to Słowacki. As for the Romantics, some of them, for instance Lord Byron, appeared to him to be seekers of truth and prophets of a humanity of the future. Romantic poetry, however, after Byron and the three Polish "bards" could not be continued on the same level and with the same intensity; certainly not in Polish, where the post-1849 decades produced either "Tyrteic" epigones like Romanowski or sentimental populists like Lenartowicz. Norwid understood this with the utmost clarity and put all his efforts into the clearing of a new path. He had no allies in his persistent search for the adequate poetic expression of essential human experience and human history. His conceptual tools were forged by Romanticism, but he sharpened them in the fire of a Christian apostolic spirit. While his own advance was slow and tortuous, he saw society continually moving away from him. Despairing over the spiritual gap created in his epoch between "progress" and "truth," Norwid was trying, as it were, with a rope-ladder of words to throw a bridge over the abyss. Contemporary critics remind one of onlookers making sarcastic comments about the poor quality of the rope-ladder or the clumsiness of Norwid's movements in trying to reach the other bank.

Norwid's conflict with the critics began in 1849 soon after the publication of a few cryptically symbolic political poems. While his first critic reproached him for the "manneristic obscurity of his thought, images, and expressions," soon it became fashionable to refer to his "queer hieroglyphs" in print, "suicidal genius" and "sickness" in private letters.[1] Neither a distant critic nor an intriguer but a friend, Bohdan Zaleski, wrote about Norwid to Jan Koźmian, a mutual acquaintance: "Norwid, as usual, strikes By-

ronic attitudes. His heart is sad and muddled . . . he won't take
advice from anyone. What a pity, for his talents are extraordinary.
Here is a powerful intellect and what's the use? He wastes his
gifts and favors; he is manneristic in his writing and behaves
strangely in everyday life." [2]

Within a year or two after he had left Rome, Norwid was already "written off" by critics and former friends and admirers
alike. The causes for this change of attitude were multiple. Norwid's confrontation with the social problems of the metropolis,
the center of a fermenting industrial society and a multilingual
emigration, the shock which he suffered from helplessly watching
the destitution and moral crisis of the "new emigration" produced
changes in him that upset many a former friend. At this juncture,
it seems, Krasiński's role was decisive. While in Rome, Norwid
was close to him and was certainly influenced by the conservative
political ideas both of the author of the *Undivine Comedy* and
his philosopher-friend Trentowski,[3] sharing with them such ideas
as the necessity of the "Christian spirit" in politics as an antidote
to revolutionary action. As the balance of power started to tilt
toward the counter-revolutionary forces, Norwid's sympathies
also began to change. A genuinely populist trend appeared in his
thinking, superseding Trentowski's pseudopopulism. Furthermore,
he now showed more understanding of the policies of the moderate Left, which wanted social reforms and supported the cause
of the oppressed nations including Poland. After standing up
against a hypnotic Mickiewicz voicing mystical and Pan-Slavic
ideas in Rome, a year later in Paris Norwid (thanks to the good
offices of his friend Chojecki, the first editorial secretary of the
Tribune des Peuples) began to see and appreciate the goodwill
and intellectual honesty of many personalities of the European
Left. He became more friendly with Mickiewicz, too.

The correspondence between Norwid and Krasiński throughout
1849 was destroyed, but we know enough of its content to be
able to reconstruct the main outlines of their differences. Krasiński
demonized Mickiewicz, regarded Chojecki as a "traitor," referred
to Paris only under the name "Babylon," and expected the worst
from everyone who set foot into this city of "Reds" and "egoists."
By the spring of 1849 he was more antirevolutionary and reactionary than ever before, despising moderates and praising military commanders like Windischgrätz and Changarnier as saviors

of European civilization.[4] Norwid's sympathy for the victims of military repression was interpreted by Krasiński as dangerous weakness. In a letter of June 1, 1849, he gave the younger poet the following advice: "Try to impress your Idea upon peoples' souls more expressively and with more clarity . . . obscurity [is] egoism. . . . You are treating them as an aristocrat. *Here* [only] you must be a Democrat!"[5] (Emphasis added.) Thus Krasiński saw his friend edging closer to the "Reds" in politics and resented his friendly contacts with Mickiewicz; on the other hand, his hermetism appeared to Krasiński (himself an obscure and cryptic poet on occasion) as asocial, almost an insult to the public. In 1850 Cieszkowski and Krasiński visited Paris where they met Norwid. Afterwards Krasiński recalled that when they had remonstrated with Norwid that he ought to write "more clearly," he just would not listen. This episode spelled the end of their regular correspondence. Krasiński, though for a while continuing to support Norwid with occasional funds, decided that his former friend was "crazy" and an "ungrateful poseur."[6]

Krasiński's influence was considerable in Polish intellectual circles, but not only he and his friends turned against Norwid. So did Jan Koźmian in Poznań and most critics and editors of Polish papers in Poznań and Cracow. Part of the problem was, of course, political. Norwid in 1849 was no longer a nice young man of vaguely idealistic or moderately conservative views, even if some of his poems still echoed Trentowski's and Krasiński's ideas. He could be regarded neither as a "regular" Catholic nor as a convert to the radical ideas of the Democrats. Poems like *Fraszka (!) I* (If Poland is not to go by the Milky Way . . .), showing the futility of absolutist political arguments, cut both ways, against conservatists and radicals simultaneously. While his Leftist populism probably irritated some of his former political friends, he was certainly not ostracized for political reasons alone. What infuriated critics and some friends was Norwid's "mannerism," his willful obscurity.

This accusation was not entirely unfounded. *Zwolon* was an experiment and turned out to be a failure. Poems such as *On the Eve of the Vigil* and *One More Word* with their esoteric political and philosophical symbolism and jagged form do not belong to the best work produced by Norwid in those years. In 1849 and 1850 he also wrote perfectly understandable poems, some of which (*Vêndome, A Song from Our Land, Anathemas*) were printed in the Poznań papers. Others, like *In Verona, Trilogy,* or *A Prayer,* remained in manuscript but were probably known to some of his detractors. Not all that he wrote was obscure, but his style, in general, must have been too complex, too demanding of intellectual effort for a reader who grew up on Niemcewicz, cherished *Pan Tadeusz,* and thought highly of Wincenty Pol. Such people, who constituted the majority of the readership around 1850, took Norwid for some sort of a crank or madman. Norwid was not unaware of this, and in a poem (*Scherzo, II*) written at the time characterized himself as the "Madman" while his friends and critics were collectively embodied in the character of the "Doctor." The latter urges the Madman to write a book, but in vain, for his "patient" already knows in advance that whatever he writes will not be understood. Other judgments which he expects to hear is

     . . . . that this matter is deep,
     That I know the language perfectly, or on the contrary:
     That I have almost completely forgotten [it]. . . .[7]

The two allegations, of course, cancel each other out; if statement A is true, statement B cannot be. A few lines later, however, the Doctor suddenly puts his finger on the sore spot:

     Because your talk is sharp—you have not trained
     The public to such language. . . .[8]

Norwid realized that his way of writing was too involved and could not be popular. What he did not realize was the almost complete isolation that would result from his experiments. As Krasiński put it in a letter in 1851: "Through him [Norwid] the Polish language is becoming ultimately asocial (*dochodzi do ostatecznego odspołecznienia*), since the social link between phrases is *Sense.*"[9] Norwid's awareness of the difficulties of communication between himself and his potential readers can be documented by statements like the following: "As to the language of society which one acquires through intercourse with the objective spirit of the given time—with the objective spirit of the public—this I was unable to acquire, which circumstance is proved by the fact that I managed to publish only those things which, so to speak, were impossible to bury and not to publish." [10] This admission brings us to the nub of the problem. Whatever difference arose between Norwid and Krasiński (whom after his death Norwid referred to as a "nobly differing friend"), or between Norwid and his editors in Poznań, the main reason for the hostile reception of Norwid's work was not subjective: it was due to the absence of a definite social group responsive to Norwid's ideas and experiments with the language. The particular groups to which Norwid related or addressed his poetic message would change with each work—sometimes it was the "young emigration," at others the whole Polish nation or even the "Christian world." Nonetheless, the most important social group which could have supported him in his endeavors, with which he could have had intellectual intercourse, the intelligentsia, still did not exist. The structure of his thought and the nature of his artistic expression define Cyprian Norwid as the first writer of the Polish intelligentsia, at the time a social group still in the process of formation.[11] In spite of his gentry origins and petty-bourgeois environment, Norwid always regarded himself as a "classless" artist or as an "intellectual worker." From a sociological point of view the story of his recognition in Poland has been the "success-story" of the whole intelligentsia as an independent and significant stratum.

Norwid's "strangeness," then, is to a large extent the expression of a discrepancy between the poetic method and form (positing a different kind of a consumer) and nineteenth-century Polish society with its traditional expectations and Romantic or Positivistic aspirations. As a precursor of Symbolism he was bound to be discovered by a generation drawn to Symbolism. But his theory of *przemilczenie* with all its consequences could appeal only to readers used to the allusiveness, fragmentariness, and "spaced out" structure of modern poetry.

Though he believed firmly in the validity of his own historiosophy and in the objective nature of truth, Norwid's *Weltanschauung* was pluralistic, and his artistic method was close to cognitive relativism.[12] As for his language, it strikes one with its deliberate eclecticism, its blend of the old and the new. It is a multistoried structure in which several different layers can be identified, beginning with the language of the Bible and the

Fathers of the Church. There is a layer of old Polish expressions or archaisms, a layer of Romanticism, of nineteenth-century philosophy, of scientific expressions translated from French, and, finally, of the language of everyday life which in Norwid's case means anything from the salon to the street. Mickiewicz's vocabulary still did not contain a Polish word for "machine"; Norwid's vocabulary even has "telegram" and "telephone." It is a language which is urban and ironic. Expressions from the sphere of "civilization" are ironically contrasted with and deflated by words with "eternal"—historical or cultural—connotations. In short, Norwid's was a partialy successful attempt to create a language for a social group which came to existence only in the last two decades of the poet's life—an extremely difficult and ungrateful task, which explains not only the hostility of his contemporaries but also his many freak-words, fiascos, and morphological and syntactic oddities of style. Speaking about the almost inevitable clash of the genuinely progressive poet with his society, Norwid raises a thought which can be applied to both the ideas of the future and its language: "For how can one, pushing society into the future and bringing it the language of future emotions, how can one clearly communicate with the present—how can one talk freely with people whose language is still being created?" [13]

Taking all this into account, Norwid's problem of finding an adequate language was rather different from that of Gerard Manley Hopkins, another innovator with whom he is often compared.[14] The neologisms and linguistic innovations of Hopkins were only adding to the precision and intensity of his feelings, while his experiment in rhythm and meter was more significant from a formal than from a social and psychological point of view. Hopkins's language is inimitable and complete in itself; Norwid's, in spite of his originality, is much more "open" and can be built upon or continued. Although some similarities can be found in their philosophy, esthetics, and religious faith, the direction and main object of their preoccupations are different. Hopkins is a "nature poet" which Norwid is not; the English Jesuit is much more circumscribed by his religious faith and isolated by his vocation than Norwid is by his historiosophy and circumstances. When we think of Norwid, we do not think of him *primarily* as a religious poet. While Hopkins's innovations are linked to medieval tradition, Norwid is not particularly interested in the

Middle Ages—he is much closer to the age of Tacitus and to the Renaissance. There is a definite similarity between Norwid and Hopkins in the posthumous fate of their work—the reluctant discovery of the "eccentric" growing into general acceptance which assigns a place of honor to the poet as the precursor of modern poetry.

We have pointed out earlier that in spite of Norwid's rebellion against Romantic convention and his anti-Romanticism, in poetic practice there were numerous links between Norwid and Romantic thought and poetry. Though he translated Homer and Dante, and greatly admired Shakespeare, Romantics such as Byron, Słowacki, Mickiewicz, and Victor Hugo influenced his style and mode of expression, while Ballanche, Cieszkowski, Libelt, Krasiński, and even Emerson contributed in varying degrees to the historiosophic content of his work. The fact that certain affinities can be detected between his and Carlyle's ideas, his and Ruskin's esthetics, and that his poetry, especially after 1851, shows traits also appearing in the poems of Browning, the Parnassians, and the French Symbolists need not lead to further speculations whether Norwid read this or that author. All that this shows is the irrefutable fact that Norwid belonged to the intellectual avant-garde of the epoch and was among the best post-Romantic poets of contemporary Western Europe.

II Rediscovery and Reappraisal

Norwid, whom a modern critic called "the most complex of all Polish artists," had a long, complicated, and intriguing history of posthumous recognition. The poet whose name in his lifetime, to quote Kraszewski, became "synonymous with eccentricity" seemed to be forgotten until 1896 when Wiktor Gomulicki made the first unsuccessful attempt to unearth his literary heritage. Soon afterwards Zenon Przesmycki (Miriam) came across Norwid's *Poems* (*Poezje*) in the Brockhaus edition and began to collect Norwidiana with the zeal of a fanatic connoisseur. He began to publish Norwid's manuscripts in the literary review *Chimera* in 1901 and devoted the rest of his life to the exacting task of collecting, sifting, and editing this truly impressive *oeuvre*. The "Norwid renaissance" initiated by Przesmycki has been going on ever since. It is another matter that while Przesmycki's work as a collector and editor of Norwid was immensely valuable, his

illness and almost morbid perfectionism delayed the publication
of the complete Norwid until after the Second World War. The
first complete edition of Norwid's *Collected Works* (*Pisma
wszystkie*), reached the Polish reader only in 1973—ninety years
after the poet's death!

Przesmycki and his contemporaries, the anti-Positivist, Nietz-
sche-loving, anarchistic Bohemians of "Young Poland," on the
whole interpreted Norwid in a manner that suited their personal
tastes and sensibilities. In this respect the title of Przesmycki's
introductory article in *Chimera* titled "The Fate of Genius" was
symptomatic. Although his poetry was admired (more admired
than understood) by the young, what impressed them above all
was Norwid's personality, his "voice in the wilderness," his ideas,
disappointments, and frustrations; he was seen as the Polish
poète maudit. Norwid's legend at this point shone brighter than
the inner glow of his art. Stanisław Wyspiański, the best playwright of the period, intuitively grasped those ideas of Norwid
which he felt he could use in his theater (e.g., the Slavic past
interpreted as a mystery-play; symbolic analogies within history),
but was too preoccupied with his own themes to draw any theoretical consequences from Norwid's writing. Only one critic,
Stanislaw Brzozowski, proposed a different approach to the author
of *Promethidion*. "Of all our writers," wrote Brzozowski, "he had
the deepest sense of history." [15] He was inspired by Norwid's
thoughts on work and interpreted Norwid's poetry as an affirma-
tion of human freedom which is fundamentally a negation of
nature. Brzozowski also emphasized the Catholic character of
Norwid's thought and his faith in the nation as a living organism,
"a living and complete form of truth." While this interpretation,
based on a close reading of the poet, was true to the facts and
not untimely before the First World War, after 1918 when independent Poland became reality it was taken up by right-wing
circles in a diluted and simplified form. In the late 1920's and
early 1930's Norwid was repeatedly discussed and tendentiously
interpreted by authors who saw political ammunition in some of
his utterances (often quoted out of context and applied to an
actual political situation) and misused by scholars whose motives for working on Norwid remain unfathomable to this day.
A case in point was the editor of the badly prepared and incom-
petently annotated one-volume edition of Norwid's writings

published in 1934, who attacked his victim as a "reactionary" having no compassion or understanding for the sufferings of the Polish nation (!) and expressed the notion that "Norwid will remain the poet of the chosen few who are fond of riddles." [16] In spite of such opinions, stunning in their old-fashioned smugness and narrow-mindedness, between the two wars Norwid became better-known and even popular in intellectual and artistic circles to the extent of becoming "the most often quoted Polish poet." Also in this period the first French translations of Norwid were published (*Cazin, Pérard*) and the first book written about him in a foreign language (Edouard Krakowski's study written in French).

Since the end of the last war two things have happened that have confirmed Norwid's position as the most important Polish poet of the second half of the nineteenth century and as *the* precursor of modern Polish poetry. First, after an argument soon after the war whether Norwid was a "correct" model for the younger generation (Marxist critics at that point thought his was an undesirable influence), the main direction of research moved from the political and theoretical to the literary-microcritical level. New studies on various aspects of Norwid's *oeuvre* as well as on such individual works as *Vade-Mecum, Quidam,* and others showed not only the complexity and richness of his texts but also the dialectical historicist nature of his thinking. Second, since Jastrun's essay entitled *The Unknown Norwid,* written in 1947, popular editions of his poetry have reached practically every literate Pole. If we discount the crippling effect of compulsory school reading, we can say that Norwid has penetrated the consciousness of the new generations. His idiosyncratic and skeptical approach to reality, implicit in the questioning of the genuineness and validity of generally accepted attitudes and values, began to attract followers, especially among the young intelligentsia. In this context the view of Zbigniew Bieńkowski, a contemporary poet and translator, seems to be particularly relevant: "For the first time our poetry—not in the declarations of the poets but in the structure of their verse—reaches back to the ancestor of Polish modernity (*nowatorstwo*), to Norwid. It is not a sacrosanct Norwid, a mystic, untouchable and mumified by respect, but a living Norwid with whom one can argue and whom one can overcome." [17]

In a sense Norwid is more alive today than any other Polish poet of the past century. Mickiewicz still can touch Polish hearts and Słowacki enchant the lovers of the Polish language, but Norwid transcends the role of a national classic on several counts. His universality, the anthropological—Hellenistic-Christian— framework of his thought, the paradoxical, ironical, unfinished, "open" aspect of his verse, the searching, eclectic yet creative, nervous, and sensitive quality of his language—all these pre-destined him to be understood only by twentieth-century man. Although even now, after Juliusz Gomulicki's painstaking re-search and careful interpretation of every poem by Norwid, there exist ambiguous and unclear passages; this critic tends to agree with Przyboś, according to whom Norwid "seen through the poetry of our century" is not hard to understand.[18] Norwid's work has its flaws, weaknesses, personal asides that interest only stu-dents of the period, obsessions that from a distance seem almost meaningless. All the same, his overall achievement is outstand-ing—and not only against the backdrop of Polish literature. As an innovator and a provider of a poetic model for the twentieth century, he stands comparison with a Browning or a Mallarmé; as a thinker he impresses with the intensity of his cultural and historical consciousness. In his lifetime he was thought of as "the poet of ruins"; today we see that he was the poet of the still unbuilt temple of the human conscience. He saw man as a maker of beauty and of history. Norwid's art is the celebration of the divine spark in man: it is the celebration of human creativity.

Notes and References

Chapter One

1. For the original text see Cyprian Norwid, *Dzieła zebrane*, this edition ed. by Juliusz W. Gomulicki, (Warsaw, 1966) I, 156. In the following, referred to as: Norwid, *DZ*.
2. *Ibid.*, p. 172.
3. Juliusz W. Gomulicki, *Wprowadzenie do biografi Norwida* (Warsaw, 1956), p. 14.
4. Norwid, *DZ*, I, 171.
5. See Norwid, *DZ* (Warsaw, 1966) II, 254. On his departure from Warsaw, several friends, including Antoni Czajkowski, wrote poems of farewell to Norwid.
6. Norwid, *DZ*, I, 198.
7. *Ibid.*, p. 204.
8. L. Orpiszewki's letter to Czartoryski was quoted by Zofia Trojanowicz in *Rzecz o młodości Norwida* (Poznań, 1968), p. 170.
9. Cf. Stanisław Szenic, *Maria Kalergis* (Warsaw, 1963), p. 197.
10. Quoted from "The People's Hands Were Swollen With Applause" in Christine Brooke-Rose's English version, *Botteghe Oscure*, XXII, Autumn 1958, p. 192.
11. Gomulicki, *Wprowadzenie*, p. 22.
12. Cyprian Norwid, *Dzieła*, ed. Tadeusz Pini (Warsaw, 1934), p. 508.
13. *Ibid.*
14. Manfred Kridl, *A Survey of Polish Literature and Culture* (The Hague, 1956), p. 77.
15. Gomulicki in *DZ*, II, 348–49.
16. Norwid, *DZ*, I, 212.
17. Cyprian Norwid, *Pisma polityczne i filozoficzne* (London 1957), p. 23.
18. Norwid, *DZ*, I, 549.

Chapter Two

1. Cyprian Norwid, *Pisma wybrane*, ed. J. W. Gomulicki (Warsaw, 1968), V, 176.

2. See Czesław Latawiec, *C. K. Norwid i jego czasy* (Poznań, 1939) in which the author devotes a whole chapter to the analysis of *Promethidion* against the background of "Platonic systems" of esthetics.
3. Both R. Zrębowicz in his introduction to a separate edition of *Promethidion* (1921) and Jan Piechocki in his *Norwidowa koncepcja sztuki-pracy* (Poznań, 1929); the latter study discusses Norwid's esthetic and social views in considerable detail and in the context of European thought.
4. Juliusz Słowacki, *Utwory wybrane*, (Warsaw, 1969), I, 252.
5. Pierre-Simon Ballanche, *Essais de Palingénésie sociale* (Paris-Geneva, 1830), p. 110.
6. Norwid, *Pisma wybrane*, II, 212.
7. *Ibid.*, p. 216.
8. Karol Libelt, *Estetyka* (Poznań, 1842), p. 323. Norwid greatly respected Libelt both as a thinker and as a man of integrity, and in 1849 when Libelt was editor of the Poznań paper *Dziennik Polski* sent him an article for publication.
9. Norwid, *Pisma wybrane*, II, 222.
10. *Ibid.*
11. Piechocki, *op. cit.*, p. 75.
12. Norwid, *Pisma wybrane*, II, 228.
13. *Ibid.*, p. 233. In fact all italicized words and expressions in quotations are Norwid's own. This is a characteristic trait of Norwid's style and as Makowiecki points out in *O Norwidzie pięć studiów* (Toruń, 1949), Norwid uses his mottos, footnotes, and typographical stresses as kinds of "emotional amplifiers," *op. ct.*, p. 15.
14. *Ibid.*, p. 241.
15. *Ibid.*, p. 243.
16. Manfred Kridl, *op. cit.*, p. 312.
17. Taduesz Makowiecki in the collection *O Norwidzie pięć studiów*, p. 31.

Chapter Three

1. Jan Błoński, "Norwid wśród prawnuków," *Twórczość*, May 1967, p. 70.
2. Norwid, *DZ*, I, 696.
3. Quoted from Christine Brooke-Rose's translation in *Botteghe Oscure*, XXII, Autumn 1958, p. 194.
4. Norwid, *DZ*, I, 545.
5. There is more than a superficial similarity between Norwid's prototype of a "lady of society" and the heroine of Bolesław Prus's novel *Lalka*. In the novel, Izabella Łęcka's social pretentions and petty intrigues cause the downfall of Wokulski.

Notes and References

6. Norwid, *DZ*, I, 547.

7. Cf. Mieczysław Jastrun's essay on *Vade-Mecum*, *Poezja*, June, 1971.

8. Introduction to the 1962 edition of *Vade-Mecum*: Cyprian Norwid, *Vade-Mecum* (Warsaw, 1962), p. 8.

9. Such was the description given by Norwid in one of his lectures on Słowacki. See Norwid, *Pisma wybrane*, IV, 256.

10. *Wszystkie pisma Cypriana Norwida*, ed. Z. Przesmycki (Warsaw, 1937), IX, 13.

11. In his introduction to the 1962 edition of *Vade-Mecum*, also in Norwid, *DZ*, II, 744 ff. He has since revised his opinion, and in the introduction to the second Warsaw edition of *Vade-Mecum* (1969), he discusses the same theory with certain qualifications, emphasizing the role of Dante as a common source of Norwid and Baudelaire.

12. Jerzy Pieterkiewicz, "Cyprian Norwid's *Vade-Mecum*: an Experiment in Didactic Verse," *The Slavonic and East European Review*, XLIV (January, 1966), 71.

13. Georges Duveau, *La vie ouvrière en France sous le Second Empire* (Paris, 1946), p. 270; as for the stagnation of real income see *ibid.*, p. 536.

14. Cyprian Norwid, *Vade-Mecum*, ed. J. W. Gomulicki, (2nd ed., Warsaw, 1969), p. 53.

15. Błoński, *op. cit.*, p. 86.

16. Norwid, *DZ*, I, 663–64. English version is quoted in Christine Brooke-Rose's translation from *Botteghe Oscure*.

17. Frank J. Corliss, Jr., "Time and Crucifixion in Norwid's *Vade-Mecum*," *The Slavic and East European Journal*, XI, no. 3 (Fall, 1967), 287.

18. *Pamięci Cypriana Norwida* (Warsaw, 1946), p. 54.

19. Błoński, *op. cit.*, p. 88.

20. Norwid, *Vade-Mecum*, 2nd ed., p. 187. The English version is quoted in Zbigniew Bieńkowski's and Sydney Smith's translation, from a collection prepared for publication by the University of Iowa Press.

21. Norwid, *Pisma wybrane*, IV, 197 and 240.

22. Maria Grzędzielska, "Wiersz Norwida w okresie *Vade mecum*," *Annales Universitatis M.C. Skłodowska*, Sectio F., XV, 1960 (Lublin, 1963), p. 119.

23. The Piasts were the first dynasty in Polish prehistory; the beginnings of their rule are surrounded by legends and popular tales.

24. Norwid, *Vade-Mecum*, 2nd ed., p. 166. The English version is in my literal translation. There exists a full English version of the poem, which was printed in *The Polish Review*, XV, no. 2, Spring, 1970.

25. Tadeusz Filip, *Fortepian Szopena* (Cracow, 1949), p. 220.

26. Norwid, *Pisma wybrane*, V, 624.
27. Norwid, *DZ*, I, 772.
28. Norwid, *Pisma wybrane*, IV, 214.
29. Norwid, *Wszystkie pisma*, IX, 219.
30. Norwid, *DZ*, I, 758.

Chapter Four

1. Norwid, *Pisma wybrane*, I, 200–01.
2. *Ibid.*, II, 129.
3. Cf. Zygmunt Zaniewicki, "Rozmyślania nad Quidam," in *Norwid żywy*, ed. B. Świderski (London, 1962), pp. 165–187.
4. Cf. his letter to General Skrzynecki, no. 35 in Norwid, *Pisma wybrane*, V, 83–85.
5. Norwid, *Pisma wybrane*, II, 157.
6. This is clear from Norwid's letters to Maria Trębicka from the United States and also from the style of his works written between 1853 and 1856.
7. Norwid, *Pisma wybrane*, II, 129.
8. *Ibid.*, p. 39.
9. J. W. Gomulicki in the introduction to Norwid, *Dwa poematy miłosne* (Warsaw, 1966), p. 19.
10. *Wielka Encyklopedia Powszechna Ilustrowana* (Warsaw, 1903), p. 571.
11. For instance, Lucjan Siemieński. His opinion is quoted in Zenon Przesmycki (Miriam), *Wybór pism krytycznych* (Cracow, 1967), II, 285.
12. *Wszystkie pisma Cypriana Norwida po dziś w całości lub fragmentach odszukane*, ed. Z. Przesmycki (Warsaw, 1938), VI, 67.
13. Victor Hugo, *La Légende des Siècles*, ed. H. J. Hunt (Oxford, 1957), p. xi.
14. Norwid, *Prisma wybrane*, II, 256.
15. *Dzieła Cyprian Norwida, ed.* Tadeusz Pini (Warsaw, 1934), p. 597.
16. Norwid, *Pisma wybrane*, II, 261.
17. *Ibid.*, p. 276.
18. Dominique de Roux, *Entretiens avec Gombrowicz* (Paris 1968), p. 68.
19. Norwid, *Pisma wybrane*, II, 79.
20. Cf. J. W. Gomulicki's introduction to Norwid, *Dwa poematy miłosne*, p. 33.
21. "Lunatyk czyli sześć wieczorów kasztelana," J. N. Kamiński, *Haliczanka czyli Zbiór nowszy wierszy* (Lwów, 1835).
22. Norwid, *Pisma wybrane*, II, 104.

Notes and References

23. M. Buczkówna, "Z przeciw-uczucia do przeciw-rozumu," *Poezja*, 1967, 5, p. 30.
24. Norwid, *Pisma wybrane*, II, 120.
25. Z. Przesmycki, *op. cit.*, p. 335.

Chapter Five

1. Norwid, *Pisma wybrane*, V, 70.
2. *Ibid.*, pp. 131–32.
3. *Ibid.*, p. 131.
4. *Ibid.*, p. 132.
5. Maria Grzędzielska, "Symbolika Zwolona," *Pamiętnik Literacki*, LIX, 4 (1968), 92.
6. *Ibid.*, p. 88.
7. Józef Ignacy Kraszewski, *Stara baśń* (Warsaw, 1948), II, 427.
8. Norwid, *Pisma wybrane*, V, 595.
9. *Ibid.*, II, 55.
10. Irena Sławińska, *O komediach Norwida* (Lublin, 1953), p. 96.
11. Norwid, *Pisma wybrane*, III, 49.
12. Norwid, *DZ*, I, 494.
13. This is an allusion to the second husband of Maria Kalergis, Sergey Muchanow, who had been the Warsaw police chief and was later personal aide-de-camp to the retired Grand Duke Constantine. Muchanow was nominated Head of the Management of all Theaters and Imperial Palaces in 1868 and was often seen in Warsaw theaters.
14. Sławińska, *op. cit.*, p. 84.
15. *Wszystkie pisma Cypriana Norwida*, ed. Z. Przesmycki, II, 231.
16. Quoted by Gomulicki in *Pisma wybrane*, V, 462.
17. Sławińska, *op. cit.*, p. 241.
18. Norwid, *Pisma wybrane*, III, 158.
19. *Ibid.*, V, 595–96.
20. August Grodzicki's opinion quoted by Gomulicki in *Pisma wybrane*, III, 472.
21. Norwid, *Pisma wybrane*, III, 440. The Polish word for infant *niemowlę* means literally "one who cannot speak"; this might have been used by Norwid in the sense of "one who cannot *yet* speak."

Chapter Six

1. Cf. Gomulicki's note in Norwid, *Pisma wybrane*, IV, 6.
2. Mickiewicz left Paris for the Middle East in 1855 to organize a Jewish Legion to fight on the side of Turkey against Russia. He died soon afterwards, probably of cholera.
3. Victor Hugo, *La Légende des Siècles* (Oxford, 1957), p. 184.
4. Mieczysław Jastrun, *Gwiaździsty diament* (Warsaw, 1971), p. 107.

5. Olga Scherer-Virski, *The Modern Polish Short Story* (The Hague, 1955), p. 48.

6. Norwid, *Pisma wybrane*, IV, 152.

7. *Ibid.*, p. 134.

8. *Ibid.*, V, 369.

9. Zbigniew Folejewski, "C. K. Norwid's Prose and the Poetics of the Short Story" in the *American Contributions to the 5th International Congress of Slavists* (The Hague, 1965), pp. 115–16.

10. Norwid, *Pisma wybrane*, IV, 203.

11. *Ibid.*, p. 205.

12. *Ibid.*, p. 209.

13. Quoted in a paraphrased version in Norwid, *Pisma wybrane*, p. 210. Part of the letter is printed by G. Wilson Knight, *Lord Byron: Christian Virtues* (London, 1952), p. 127.

14. *Norwid, op. cit.*, p. 211.

15. *Ibid.*, p. 235

16. *Ibid.*, p. 241.

17. *Ibid.*, p. 254.

18. *Ibid.*, p. 301.

19. Georg Lukács, *The Historical Novel* (Penguin, 1969), pp. 215–16.

20. Norwid, *Pisma wybrane*, V, 577–78. *Czamarka* is a Polish-style overcoat. This allusion indicates that the person in question was also a Pole.

21. *Ibid.*, p. 688.

Chapter Seven

1. Norwid, *Pisma wybrane*, II, 299.

2. *Ibid.*, p. 290.

3. *Ibid.*, p. 294.

4. Zdzisław Lapiński, *Norwid* (Warsaw, 1971), p. 105.

5. Norwid, *Pisma wybrane*, V, 144.

6. *Ibid.*, p. 330.

7. See Marian Kubiel, *Dzieje Polski porozbiorowe*, 2nd ed. (London, 1963), p. 413.

8. Norwid's *Pisma wybrane*, V, 152.

9. Norwid, *DZ*, I, 566.

10. *Ibid.*, p. 456.

11. The most recent of these was Alicja Lisiecka's "Z problemów historyzmu Cypriana Norwida" in *Pamiętnik Literacki*, L. 2, 1959, and the same author's "Romantyczna 'Filozofia przyszłości' Cypriana Norwida," offprint from *Nowe studia o Norwidzie* (Warsaw, 1961).

12. Cyprian Norwid, *Pisma polityczne i filozoficzne* (London, 1957), p. 29. For Hegel the state stood for "the realization of free-

Notes and References

dom." Hegel's theory of the state is discussed in detail in Herbert Marcuse, *Reason and Revolution* (Boston, 1960), p. 214.

13. Norwid, *Pisma polityczne i filozoficzne*, p. 42.
14. Norwid, *Pisma wybrane*, V, 464.
15. *Ibid.*, p. 202.
16. *Ibid.*, p. 201.
17. Nicholas Berdayev, *Slavery and Freedom* (New York, 1944), p. 171. In this context, of course, Solovyev's views can be quoted as well, for he influenced Berdayev.
18. Łapiński, *op. cit.*, p. 131.
19. Norwid, *Pisma wybrane*, V, 202.
20. *Ibid.*, p. 318.
21. Norwid, *DZ*, I, 507.
22. Norwid, *Pisma wybrane*, V, 456.
23. *Ibid.*, p. 277.
24. *Ibid.*, p. 437.
25. *Ibid.*, pp. 460 and 465.
26. *Ibid.*, p. 531.
27. *Ibid.*, p. 543.
28. Norwid, *DZ*, I, 387.
29. *Ibid.*, p. 396.
30. Norwid, *Pisma polityczne i filozoficzne*, p. 21.
31. See his letter to Zaleski in Norwid, *Pisma wybrane*, V, 88.
32. *Ibid.*, p. 255.
33. Norwid, *Pisma polityczne i filozoficzne*, p. 167.
34. *Ibid.*, p. 169.
35. *Ibid.*, p. 169.
36. Norwid, *DZ*, I, 524.
37. *Ibid.*, p. 637.

Chapter Eight

1. The first quotation is from W. Bentkowski; the rest are from J. Klaczko, *Pisma z lat 1849–1851* (Poznań, 1919), p. 35, and from a quotation in Norwid, *Pisma wybrane*, I, 97.
2. *Korespondencya J. B. Zaleskiego* (Lwów, 1911), II, 128; also quoted by Gomulicki in Norwid, *DZ*, II, 368.
3. Krasiński and B. F. Trentowski were co-authors of a book, *Przedburza polityczna* (Frieburg, 1848), published under Trentowski's name. Norwid read this book while in Rome and it influenced his political thinking at the time.
4. Windischgrätz broke the resistance of revolutionary Vienna in October, 1848; Changarnier was the successor of General Cavaignac, the Minister of War in June, 1848. Though Changarnier did not become as notorious as Cavaignac, he was also unpopular in reformist

and radical circles. In Victor Hugo's words, he was a *"Jésuite à épaulettes."* Cf. V. Hugo, *Souvenirs personelles 1848–1851*, (Paris, 1952), p. 277.

5. Quoted in Dr. Stanisław Kossowski, *Krasiński a Norwid* (Lwów, 1912), p. 48.
6. *Ibid.*, p. 52.
7. Norwid, *DZ*, I, 272.
8. *Ibid.*, p. 273.
9. *Ibid.*, p. lvii.
10. Norwid, *Pisma wybrane*, V, 138.
11. Zdzisław Łapiński, *Norwid* (Cracow, 1971), p. 156.
12. *Ibid.*, p. 161.
13. Norwid, *Pisma wybrane*, IV, 249. Also quoted by Łapiński in *op. cit.*, p. 164.
14. See J. Pieterkiewicz, "Introducing Norwid," *Slavonic and East European Review*, XXVII, no. 68 (December, 1948), pp. 228–47, and Jolanta W. Zielińska, "Norwid i Hopkins," *Oficyna Poetów*, I, 1, pp. 15–21.
15. St. Brzozowski, *Legenda Młodej Polski* (2nd ed., Lwów, 1910), p. 199.
16. Tadeusz Pini, Introduction to *Dzieła Cypriana Norwida* (Warsaw, 1934), p. xlv.
17. Zbigniew Bieńkowski, *Modelunki* (Warsaw, 1966), p. 520.
18. Quoted in Norwid, *Pisma wybrane*, I, 122.

Selected Bibliography

BIBLIOGRAPHIES

BOROWY, WACLAW. Bibliografia Norwida. In Muzeum Narodowe, *Pamięci Cypriana Norwida*. Warsaw: 1946.
NORWID, CYPRIAN, in *Bibliografia Literatury Polskiej. Nowy Korbut. Romantyzm. Hasła osobowe K-O*. Ed. Irmina Śliwińska and Stanisław Stupkiewicz. Warsaw: PIW, 1969, pp. 448–514.

PRIMARY SOURCES

Pisma zebrane. Vol. A (Parts 1–2), C, E, ed. Z. Przesmycki. Warsaw-Cracow, 1911–1913; Vol. F., Cracow, 1946. This is the first extensive selection from Norwid's work, Vol. A consisting of both lyric and epic poetry, Vol. C of dramatic writings and Vol. E of prose writings. Vol. F contains Norwid's writings on art and literature; although prepared for publication already in 1914, it was published only in 1946 with Wacław Borowy's foreword. Vols. B, D, G, and H were never published. All volumes are accompanied by notes and commentaries by Z. Przesmycki.
Wszystkie pisma Cypriana Norwida po dziś w całości lub fragmentach odszukane. Vols. 3–9. Ed. Z. Przesmycki. Warsaw, 1937–39. Vols. 3–4 contain Norwid's plays, 5 his prose writings, 6 his essays and articles on art and literature, 8–9 his correspondence. This is the most complete edition of Norwid's work prior to the Second World War. Its special importance lies in the publication of Norwid's letters, for the first time collected in a book. Vol. 7 was already at the printer's when war broke out and the entire edition perished with the exception of one copy. It was eventually published on the basis of this proofread copy by Z. Zaniewicki: Cyprian Norwid, *Pisma polityczne i filozoficzne*, London, 1957 with Zaniewicki's afterword.
Dzieła zebrane. Vols. 1–2 (1. Wiersze. Tekst. 2. Wiersze. Dodatek krytyczny.) Ed. Juliusz W. Gomulicki. Warsaw: PIW, 1966. The first vols. of a critical edition planned for six vols., since then abandoned or adjourned indefinitely. Vol. 1 contains a long in-

troduction by Gomulicki and a chronicle of Norwid's life and work (also published separately by PIW under the title *Wprowa-dzenie do biografii Norwida*) and 371 lyrical poems. The greater part of Vol. 2 is taken up by Comulicki's commentaries to the poems. These, though useful in clearing up many obscure parts in the more difficult poems, have been criticized as "controversial." Gomulicki tries to link most allusions with details of Norwid's biography. The editor's changes in Norwid's interpunction and his modernization of spelling are also debatable.

Pisma wybrane. Vols. 1–5. Selected and edited by J. W. Gomulicki. Warsaw: PIW, 1968. This selection was brought out to meet the nonspecialist readers' demand. Vol. 1 contains lyrical verse, 2 longer and epic poems (with some regrettable cuts in *Quidam* and in *Rzecz o wolności słowa*), 3 *dramas* (omitting the "dramatic miniatures"), 4 prose works, and 5 letters. Apart from an introduction by Gomulicki and a calendar of Norwid's life, there is an appendix quoting contemporaries' and critics' opinion on various works by Norwid. Gomulicki's notes are short and not always adequate; his glossary to Norwid's neologisms at the end of each volume is useful.

Pisma wszystkie. Vols. 1–10 and supplementary vol. Ed. J. W. Gomulicki. Warsaw: PIW, 1971–1974. The first complete edition of all Norwid's writings. It contains all the poetic and prose fragments that have come to light since 1939, including 75 letters written to Norwid by other persons. In 1971 nine vols. were published, the last two and the supplementary volume (containing the editor's afterword and reproductions of Norwid's drawings) appeared during 1972–74.

SECONDARY SOURCES

In Polish

ARCIMOWICZ, WLADYSLAW. *Cyprian Kamil Norwid na tle swego konfliktu z krytyką.* Wilno, 1935. An interesting critical study looking into the causes of the hostile reception of Norwid's work by his contemporaries. It contains insights into Norwid's psychology and political thinking, but its presentation of Norwid as "a mystic" is based more on speculation than on textual analysis.

BEREŻYNSKI, KAZIMIERZ. "Filozofja Cypryjana Norwida." *Sfinks,* 1911, nos. 38–41. Offprint: Warsaw, 1911. Discussion of Norwid's philosophy and historiosophy, mainly based on *Rzecz o wolności słowa* and *Milczenie.* Points out contacts with Mickiewicz's and Libelt's views but erroneously connects Norwid's thought with French traditionalism of the de Maistre type.

Selected Bibliography

BOROWY, WACLAW. *O Norwidzie*. Warsaw: PIW, 1960. A collection of essays on Norwid and reviews on Norwidiana by the well-known literary historian. Most interesting is an essay on the main motifs in Norwid's poetry.

GOMULICKI, JULIUSZ W., and JAN ZYGMUNT JAKUBOWSKI, eds. *Nowe studia o Norwidzie*. Warsaw: PWN, 1961. A collection of ten essays on Norwid and of an archivist's study on autographs of Norwid's letters in the National Library. The contributors include poets (Jastrun, Przyboś) as well as scholars (Libera, Straszewska, Szmydtowa). The essays deal with Norwid's poetry, esthetics, and historiosophic views, often in a comparativistic context.

GÓRSKI, KONRAD, TADEUSZ MAKOWIECKI, and IRENA SLIWINSKA. *O Norwidzie pięć studiów*. Toruń, 1949. A collection of essays by three distinguished scholars on various aspects of Norwid's work, including a very perceptive study on *Promethidion* by T. Makowiecki.

GÜNTHER, WLADYSLAW, ed. *Norwid żywy*. London: Świderski, 1962. A collection of essays under the auspices of the Polish Writers' Association in Exile. The level of contributions varies considerably; some essays deal with details of Norwid's biography, others discuss his overall achievement or particular aspects of his work. W. Folkierski's essay "Norwidowe inferno amerykańskie" was followed by an interesting rejoinder by Wiktor Weintraub in *Kultura* (Paris) no. 4 (1963), pp. 39–62.

JASTRUN, MIECZYSLAW. *Gwiaździsty diament*. Warsaw: PIW, 1971. Essays written on Norwid by one of the leading Polish poets in the course of twenty-four years. These include popular introductions of Norwid, polemics, and scholarly (but also poetic) interpretations of individual works. It shows much intuitive understanding of Norwid's work.

KOLACZKOWSKI, STANISLAW. "Ironia Norwida." Droga, no. 11 (1933), also included in the same author's *Pisma wybrane. Vol. I. Portrety i zarysy literackie*. Ed. Stanisław Pigoń. Warsaw: PIW, 1968. An excellent study on irony, a central component in Norwid's poetry. The non-Romantic character of this irony is stressed and its social origins traced from the rules of conduct of the nineteenth-century *salon*.

KRECHOWIECKI, ADAM. *O Cyprianie Norwidzie. Próba charakterystyki. Przyczynki do obrazu życia i prac poety, na podstawie źródeł rękopiśmiennych*. Lwów, 1909. Norwid's first biography, based largely on writings and letters then still unpublished or inaccessible. Today it has only a documentary value.

ŁAPINSKI, ZDZISLAW. *Norwid*. Cracow: Wyd. Znak, 1971. An intelligent introduction to Norwid's poetry from an "enlightened Catholic" point of view. It investigates the central themes, motifs, and ideas in Norwid's poetic works and shows his conflict with his readers in a new, more "sociological" light.

SŁAWIŃSKA, IRENA. *O komediach Norwida.* Lublin, 1953. A detailed discussion of Norwid's comedies, including their draft versions. Somewhat verbose, but thorough and informative.

————. *Reżyserska ręka Norwida.* Cracow: Wyd. Lit., 1971. Essays discussing various aspects of Norwid's theater. Sensitively written, it shows understanding of Norwid's stagecraft and his poetic as well as dramatic devices.

TROJANOWICZ, ZOFIA. *Rzecz o młodości Norwida.* Poznan: Wyd. Poz., 1968. Written originally as a doctoral thesis for Poznań University, this study discusses Norwid's first creative decade (1840–1850) within the context of his generation. *Zwolon* is analyzed as a "drama of this generation." The Appendix describes Norwid's contacts with Czartoryski and the Hotel Lambert on the basis of newly found letters.

WYKA, KAZIMIERZ. *Cyprian Norwid, poeta i sztukmistrz.* Cracow: Polska Akademia Umiejętności, 1948. Wyka investigates here the influence of other branches of art on Norwid's poetry. Separate chapters deal with sculpture, music, and painting; in the final chapter Norwid's artistic method is compared with that of Théophile Gautier.

In English

FOLEJEWSKI, ZBIGNIEW. "C. K. Norwid's prose and the poetics of the short story." Preprint from *American Contributions to the 5th International Congress of Slavists.* The Hague: Mouton and Co.

GÖMÖRI, GEORGE. "The Poet and the Hero. Genesis and Analysis of Norwid's *Bema Pamięci Żałobny-Rapsod." California Slavic Studies,* Vol. IV, 1967.

KRIDL, MANFRED. *A Survey of Polish Literature.* The Hague: Mouton and Co., 1956. A Chapter on Cyprian Norwid: pp. 36–14.

PIETRKIEWICZ, JERZY. "Introducing Norwid." *The Slavonic and East European Review,* XXVII, no. 68., December, 1948.

————. "Cyprian Norwid's *Vade-mecum:* An Experiment in Didactic Verse." *The Slavonic and East European Review,* XLIV, no. 102, January, 1966.

WEINTRAUB, WIKTOR. "Norwid-Pushkin. Norwid's 'Spartacus' and the Onegin stanza." *Harvard Slavic Studies,* 1954 and offprint.

Index

Index